DR TOM DAVIES

SELF
OBSESSION

How our need for identity
threatens our wellbeing

WATKINS
Sharing Wisdom
Since 1893

Self Obsession
Tom Davies

This edition first published in the UK and USA in 2025 by
Watkins, an imprint of Watkins Media Limited
Unit 11, Shepperton House
89-93 Shepperton Road
London
N1 3DF

enquiries@watkinspublishing.com

1 2 3 4 5 6 7 8 9 10

Typeset by Lapiz

Printed and bound by CPI Group (UK) Ltd, Croydon, CR0 4YY

The manufacturer's authorised representative in the EU for product safety is:
eucomply OÜ - Pärnu mnt 139b-14, 11317 Tallinn, Estonia,
hello@eucompliancepartner.com, www.eucompliancepartner.com

A CIP record for this book is available from the British Library

ISBN: 978-1-78678-950-1 (Paperback)
ISBN: 978-1-78678-951-8 (eBook)

www.watkinspublishing.com

MIX
Paper | Supporting
responsible forestry
FSC® C171272
FSC
www.fsc.org

For my family, especially my parents, who patiently read and re-read countless chapters and endured my existential philosophizing, and to my nieces and nephews, who continually remind me of what's important.

CONTENTS

INTRODUCTION

In my twenties I found myself at a crossroads with the choice of two paths, neither of which I wanted to take. The first option was to continue along the road I was already on. Let's call it The Road of Great Purpose. This path promised meaning, status and success. It would lead me to where I'd always dreamed of going. However, the journey would be fraught with anxiety and stress. The second option was an alternative path that would allow me to escape the relentless pressure and expectations. But this freedom would come at a cost – the loss of Great Purpose. I've come to know this second path as The Road of Emptiness. At the time, it felt like a no-win situation. Staying the course would be painful but changing direction might be even worse. If the choice was between living a meaningful life with anxiety or a meaningless life without it, there was only ever one path I was willing to take. I was a determined, ambitious twenty-something with big dreams and an insatiable desire to prove myself. I was committed to The Road of Great Purpose and prepared to face any obstacles that I might encounter en route.

My Great Purpose was to qualify as a doctor. This was all that mattered to me and the endless study, punishing exams and gruelling rotas did little to dampen my enthusiasm. However, it wasn't just the rigours of medical school that I was contending with. I also struggled with crippling self-doubt and severe anxiety. This anxiety manifested in various ways, from panic attacks to debilitating pre-exam nerves. I recall one four-hour clinical exam where I was so frightened that I experienced chest pain. I later learnt that it was "soldier's angina", something first observed in soldiers on the battlefield. The terror of being under sustained enemy attack caused their hearts to beat so hard that their bodies couldn't keep up with the oxygen demand. For me, the exam hall was my battlefield and the fear of failure was my enemy. It was an enemy that was ready to ambush me at every opportunity – an enemy I was powerless to escape.

The constant anxiety meant that my years of training were some of the toughest of my life. I hoped that as my medical competency grew my worries would lessen. Instead, the pressure only seemed to intensify with each passing year as the stakes kept rising. I never really considered life beyond medical school. It seemed like such a fragile dream that even thinking about it might somehow make it less likely. Besides, my panic attacks had become so frequent that day-to-day survival was about all I could manage. Worse than the panic attacks was the agoraphobia that drove me to avoid public transport, classrooms and lecture halls. This was hardly conducive to student life. I'd sometimes walk more than two hours across London for a tutorial, only to find I was too anxious to attend it. For classes I couldn't avoid, I'd drink a couple of beers beforehand. The Dutch courage would just about keep the panic attacks at bay but meant nine o'clock classes involved a particularly bleak breakfast routine.

I don't know how I got through medical school but somehow I did. It should have been a proud moment but all I felt was relief. I was exhausted and immediately consumed by the reality of what my success meant. I was now a doctor and I felt totally unprepared for what was to come. Within weeks I took my first shifts in a busy London hospital. Like many other newly qualified doctors I felt completely out of my depth. My anxiety levels were worse than ever before. My hands shook when I tried to cannulate patients and my voice trembled when I spoke to senior colleagues. I felt weak and pathetic. One medical registrar even nicknamed me "Smiler" because he took sadistic pleasure in pointing out how miserable I looked. He could see in my face what I felt inside. The stress was too much to conceal. I overheard nurses questioning my competency and saw them sniggering when consultants quizzed me on medical knowledge I was too anxious to remember.

The next two years were hell. My stethoscope felt like a noose tightening around my neck with every passing week. I should have quit but I couldn't. I had come too far to turn back. Every day I edged closer to mental collapse. I could feel my medical career slipping through my fingers and I felt helpless to stop it. The Road of Great Purpose had become a desperate limp toward a finish line that seemed to keep moving further away. The combination of fear, dread and emotional exhaustion created a trance-like existence. I was so numb that even my panic attacks stopped. I spent my commutes on the London Underground in a catatonic state, staring blankly at the floor. The Road of Great Purpose had become a living nightmare that my ego wouldn't let me wake up from. My career was all-consuming. Every waking moment was spent either working or thinking about work. I'd wake up during the night panicking that I hadn't prescribed a fictional drug for a fictional patient. On one occasion I woke up, showered and walked to the bus stop only to realize it was one in the morning and I'd slept for just half an hour. My exhaustion was such that sleep made little difference to how I felt. I was never fully awake or asleep.

But there is only so much any of us can take, no matter how determined we are. Even the deadliest pathogens need a host. The ego feeds on the spirit and one morning I woke up to find mine was broken. I walked into the emergency department for a shift and knew it was over. I couldn't face another patient. I had nothing more to give. I went into my consultant's room, broke down in tears and simply said,

"I'm done." The Road of Great Purpose had led to a dead-end and I bowed out in a not-so-glorious defeat, crying in a hospital office. I went to work that day as a doctor and left as a defeated nobody.

Of course, I wasn't a "nobody" but that's how I felt at the time. It was ego death and not the healthy, spiritually awakened kind. My perceived failure left a chasm in my life that I didn't know how to fill. I was painfully aware of the friendships I'd lost, relationships I was unable to commit to and hobbies I no longer had. The total absence of meaning in my life meant only one thing. I was now on the path I'd never dared to follow – The Road of Emptiness. It was a road that welcomed me with open arms.

The Road of Emptiness is known by many names. Each traveller has their own way of describing it. For me it meant wandering aimlessly through a dense fog of depression, accompanied by a profound sense of hopelessness and apathy that made me nostalgic for the anxiety I'd left behind – the Good Old Days where life had meaning. In fact, I felt such emptiness that I repeatedly tried to return to work as a doctor. I wanted to go down fighting rather than wither away into insignificance. I applied for various jobs I knew I'd hate, had interviews I didn't want to attend and was offered jobs that would likely have ended in my psychological ruin. Fortunately, every time I was close to accepting a job, something stopped me. There was a voice deep inside that told me in no uncertain terms that I mustn't go back – that I shouldn't suffer anymore. I was just going to have to make do with what I had.

What I had was time. Time to discover that "nothingness" wasn't the absence of everything. After a period of intense grief, dominated by bitterness, self-blame and self-pity, something else emerged from the emptiness. It was a need to understand why this had happened to me. I needed to know why I had been so anxious and why I was now so depressed. I couldn't accept that my anxiety and depression were two

4

separate issues. I was sure that there was one fundamental problem that gave rise to both. I also knew intuitively that this was the same problem that other people were struggling with. I saw it in every patient who was suffering psychologically, regardless of what specific mental health disorder they were presenting with. Now, I had to find out what it was.

I bought self-help book after self-help book, looking for clues that would point me in the right direction. I studied the works of famous psychotherapists and psychologists hoping to find a theory that offered a convincing explanation. But nothing I read brought me any closer to the truth. Some ideas seemed too simple while others were unnecessarily complicated. Was my distress really caused by a disharmony between my conscious and unconscious mind? Was I suffering from repressed desires or struggling to integrate different parts of my psyche? Maybe I was but none of these ideas resonated with me. With my bookshelf full of books I disagreed with I decided to change my approach and began exploring philosophy. It was here that I found what I was looking for – in what for me was an unlikely place – Buddhism.

I'm not a religious person. I never have been. I grew up in a loosely Catholic family but hated having to attend church. I quickly labelled myself a student of science and dismissed anything that might be considered religious or spiritual as irrational and unfounded. I had heard of Buddhism but knew very little about it and assumed it was simply another religion I wouldn't agree with. I would have probably avoided it completely if it wasn't for the existential crisis I found myself in. But by this point, I had nothing to lose. So, with scepticism, I started reading some introductory Western commentaries on Buddhism. Quickly, my scepticism turned to curiosity and this curiosity deepened with every chapter and book I read.

I was shocked by how much I could relate to the ideas. It soon became apparent that Buddhist teachings were nothing like the Bible stories I had been forced to study at Sunday School. I realized that Buddhism wasn't really a religion at all. There was no God or creator I had to believe in. What's more, the teachings focused on the very problem I had been looking to understand. And what I was reading made logical sense – much more so than many of the abstract theories in psychology or the medical spiel I used to give my patients. The more I read the closer I felt I was getting to the truth. Over the next few years, I explored various other Eastern philosophies including Taoism and Hinduism. I was shocked by how similar many of the ideas were and grew increasingly convinced that all were pointing toward the same truth. But despite my growing conviction, I wasn't ready to totally abandon Western ideas around mental health. Even though I could see flaws in the psychiatric and psychological models, I was unwilling to dismiss them entirely. I knew, for example, that anti-depressants helped many people suffering from anxiety and depression. I had taken these medications myself and prescribed them to my patients to good effect. Similarly, I knew the value of psychotherapy and counselling. There was also a huge amount of scientific research supporting these Western approaches that I couldn't overlook. I was left with an uncomfortable paradox. I knew the Eastern ideas were right but I couldn't explain why the Western methods worked since they seemed at odds with Eastern thought, both in terms of what they considered to be the underlying problem and how this problem should be treated.

Two years later, while walking in a forest in Norfolk, I had the eureka moment I had been waiting for. It was a sudden insight in which East and West came together into a single theory. I knew immediately that I had identified the problem responsible for the psychological distress that each of us experiences in our lives. It was never the case that Western psychology and Eastern philosophy were in opposition. They just understand the problem in different ways and therefore approach it from different perspectives.

Imagine your car breaks down and you take it to two different mechanics. Both recognize there is an issue with the brake system. The first mechanic believes the problem lies primarily with the brakes themselves and replaces them. The second mechanic also notices the faulty brakes but considers this a secondary issue linked to a fault in the car's hydraulics, so focuses on that instead. Similarly, a therapist or doctor might view anxiety or depression as the main problem and look to treat it directly. In contrast, Eastern philosophy would consider these issues as symptoms of a deeper, more fundamental problem. While both Western and Eastern methods strive to relieve distress, they disagree on where the main difficulty lies. This has important implications regarding the long-term success of these approaches since failing to address the underlying cause could leave people vulnerable to the recurrence of their problem. This likely explains why so many patients experience relapse after their therapy ends or anti-depressants are stopped.

The Western model is effective in fixing the acute problems it is designed to fix. However, these problems are secondary to a more fundamental issue – one that medicine and psychology simply don't recognize. The critical flaw in the Western approach is that it pulls out the weed but leaves its root behind. The root is self-obsession. This is *the problem* beneath the other problems that we must overcome if we want to be free. Self-obsession is the cause of anxiety, depression, existential angst and grief. It is self-obsession that makes the human condition inherently painful. Overcome self-obsession and you will overcome everything else.

My journey to understanding self-obsession began with my own pain. I have suffered from self-obsession and I have seen the same suffering in others. I have played the role of both patient and doctor. I lost my faith in science and found a deeper truth in spirituality. I then discovered a path that unites both. Today, I no longer suffer from depression and I am free from anxiety. I work as a therapist and I recognize the unmistakable symptoms of self-obsession in every client that I work with. It is the same self-obsession I see in my family and friends. It underpins the distress caused by psychological illnesses as well as the discomfort that is part and parcel of everyday life.

Self-obsession is everyone's problem because everybody is self-obsessed, to a greater or lesser extent, including you. And you're my reason for writing this book. I want to help you understand your own self-obsession. I want to show you how to live a happier and more fulfilling life. To do this you must first understand the problem. In Part 1 of this book, I'll explain what self-obsession is and why it's responsible for the psychological pain you experience in your life. I'll show you how your conscious awareness gave rise to self-awareness and how your relationship with your self sets you up to suffer. I'll then present the critical link between self-obsession and mental illness, demonstrating how anxiety and depression are two facets of the same problem. In Part 2 I'll provide you with everything you need to overcome self-obsession and free yourself from psychological pain.

This is not a self-help book in the traditional sense. Self-help books tend to encourage self-growth and self-development. I will advocate for neither of these things. This is because it's the "self" of "*self*-help" that's at the heart of the problem. It is the self that dragged me along The Road of Great Purpose and it's the self that refused The Road of Emptiness. The problem is self-obsession and to overcome it we must strive for *less* self, not *more*. My aim is to help *you*, not your *self*. In fact, I want to save you *from* your self. Free from your self, The Road of Emptiness becomes The Road of *Great* Emptiness. It's a path of unlimited possibilities where you'll never get lost for the simple reason that there's no destination you're trying to get to. If you're not afraid you cannot be anxious, and if you're content with how things are you cannot be depressed. These are the secrets waiting for you on the other side of self-obsession. The only question you must ask yourself is, are you ready to let your self go? If the answer is yes, then this book is for you. I hope that it gives you what it has given me.

PART I

WHAT MAKES US HUMAN?

You and I have almost certainly never met. I know nothing about you. I don't know what made you pick up this book or how you're feeling. I don't know anything about the challenges in your life or things you've been through. And yet, if we met, we'd instantly recognize a "sameness" that unites us. There's an unmistakable quality that both of us share, regardless of our individual circumstances. It's something each of us has, which we know intuitively is exclusively human. It's what gives rise to the so-called "human condition", including the psychological pain that all of us experience in our lives.

For us to understand why we suffer in the manner that we do, we must start by answering a fundamental question. "How are we different to other animals?" It's the kind of question that, at first glance, seems relatively straightforward. However, when it comes to articulating what exactly it is that sets us apart from other animals, we might find ourselves struggling. This is because so many of our "human" qualities can be seen throughout the animal kingdom.

The Wonder of Nature

Like humans, many animal species live in complex social groups. For example, wolves form communities with clear hierarchies. They live cooperatively in a pack, working together to hunt, raise their young and defend their territory. Each wolf has its role and social rank that contributes to the overall dynamics and functioning of the group. Pack harmony is maintained by the wolves' ability to communicate. They use a combination of vocalizations, including howling, body language and scent marking to communicate, allocate and coordinate tasks. This highlights the sophisticated social structures within wolf packs and also demonstrates intelligence.

Often, we think of intelligence as something which distinguishes us from other animals. However, there are many examples in the natural world where species display advanced cognitive abilities, problem-solving skills and a capacity to learn. This is perhaps best seen in our nearest relatives, chimpanzees. Most of us have seen videos of chimps using sticks and leaves as tools to extract termites from their nests. You may also be aware that some killer whales have learnt that if they strike their tails in unison, they can create a wave to displace a seal from an ice floe. This shows remarkable teamwork and an ability to problem solve to increase hunting success. Their success rate improves over time as whales learn from past experiences.

There is something even more "human" that we can observe in animals and that is their capacity to show emotions. Like us, animals can show joy, fear, anger and affection. They also display behaviours suggestive of complex emotions such as grief and empathy. I remember watching a nature documentary that followed a family of elephants during a severe drought. The matriarch led the herd hundreds of miles in search of food and water. At one point, they came across the remains of a dead elephant that had fallen victim to the drought. I watched with amazement as they gently picked up and examined the bones with their trunks. As the camera showed a close-up of one of the elephant's eyes, I was sure I could see genuine sadness. I was deeply moved by how the animal appeared to be grieving the loss of another of its kind.

This emotional intelligence can also be seen in our homes in the way our pets behave. I remember one occasion when I was sitting on my sofa crying and, recognizing that I was distressed, my dog came over and rested her head on my lap. She may not have understood why I was upset but she definitely sensed that I was and responded by providing gentle comfort. It's no coincidence that we form strong bonds with our pets. They are more than simply animals we share our homes with: they become a part of our families.

Nature's Vacuum

When we compare ourselves with other species, we find there are many more similarities than differences. Trying to distinguish us based on the human-like qualities I have just described feels somehow incomplete. Sure, you might argue that we are *more* intelligent, *more* sociable and *more* empathic but this doesn't provide a clear and concrete distinction. This is because there's something we have which goes beyond behaviour and cognition.

I was last reminded of this "elusive quality" a few months ago when I visited a local zoo with three of my nieces and nephews. On the way in the car, we discussed which animals we were most excited to see. One animal we all agreed on was the leopard and we made a beeline for the enclosure as soon as we arrived.

As luck would have it, the cats were only a few metres away from the viewing area. As we stood watching with our faces pressed against the glass, my nephew said, "I wonder what they're thinking". One of my nieces thought they were thinking about what they'd be having for lunch. I said they might be wondering why strange-looking humans were staring at them. My eldest niece said, "I don't think they're thinking about anything". After a few seconds, my nephew then said, "Maybe they don't even know we're here!". "They *must* know we're here", I said, reading the information panel at the entrance to the leopards' enclosure. "It says here that their sense of smell is 10,000 times more sensitive than ours and they can even see in the dark!"

It's the kind of wonderfully simple conversation that we might have with children that touches on deeply philosophical topics. As adults we sometimes roll our eyes and smile at the innocent words of youth, but these questions are worth taking seriously!

I had no doubt the leopards were aware of us standing on the other side of the glass. They were probably more aware of us than we were of them. However, as we watched them, we were aware that we were watching them. The same could not be said for the leopards.

This may sound strange but it's actually true of all animals. They're not aware that they're aware. In other words, they're not *consciously aware*. This means that the dramatic scenes we see unfolding in nature documentaries occur in a "conscious awareness vacuum". The lions don't know they're chasing the antelopes and the antelopes don't know they're being chased. We can't even deduce that the antelopes run because they want to live. This is because they aren't even aware that they're alive!

You might think I'm being unfair. How can the incredibly complex behaviours demonstrated by some animals occur without conscious awareness? Can a chimpanzee really learn intricate tool use without knowing it's learning? Can an elephant grieve without knowing it's grieving? As unlikely as it seems, there's no compelling evidence to suggest animals have anywhere near the conscious awareness that's seen in humans. It is this mysterious "meta" awareness that truly distinguishes us from other species.

Becoming Consciously Aware

If this is hard to get your head around, don't worry. If you're confused, the fact that you're aware of your confusion is an example of our human awareness in action! Let me explain it a little more. Right now, you're reading this book and aware you're reading this book. You also know whether you agree with my unromantic take on the animal kingdom! This is because you're consciously aware. It's such a fundamental aspect of our human experience that we tend to totally overlook it. However, you were not born consciously aware and you're not consciously aware for every hour of the day. This is because each night while you sleep, you're not aware you're sleeping. Similarly, there may be certain activities that you are so accustomed to doing that you find yourself doing them unconsciously. Have you ever been driving somewhere and realized that you don't remember the last few miles of the journey? Have you ever found yourself standing in the shower unsure of whether you've washed your hair yet or not? I know I have! We experience unconscious awareness every day but its very nature means we can never fully grasp what it's like as we don't know it has happened until we become consciously aware again.

Animals are effectively sleeping even when they're awake. Their brains are on autopilot and they're oblivious to what's happening in their lives. This was also true for you when you were a baby. You didn't know when you were hungry. You didn't know when you were cold. You never made a conscious decision to cry and you weren't aware of what was needed to make you stop.

Conscious awareness develops in children gradually over the first couple of years of life. There's no sudden "eureka" moment when a child announces, "I think therefore I am!" Instead, conscious awareness emerges like a slowly lifting fog in such a way that the child doesn't notice the change. Their brains are continuously acclimatizing to greater and greater levels of conscious awareness until they reach the complex depths of perception that you and I experience today.

A similar gradual awakening would have happened from an evolutionary perspective. Our ancestors would have become increasingly consciously aware over time. But how chance genetic mutations led to the spark of conscious awareness is one of life's greatest mysteries. Somehow, the human brain started to become aware of itself. When exactly this happened is difficult to determine but it may have actually occurred surprisingly recently and remarkably quickly, at least by evolutionary standards. This is supported by archaeological and anthropological studies that have shown rapid changes in the size of the brains of *homo sapiens* (our species!) over the last few hundred thousand years. Studies also indicate that during the same time period there was an explosion of more complex behaviours, like cultural and ceremonial practices. These findings are likely all signs of our ancestors' rapidly increasing conscious awareness.

While the emergence of conscious awareness remains a hotly debated topic, it's easy to see how being consciously aware would have given early humans a significant survival advantage. It would have made them better equipped to respond to potential threats, more adept at problem solving and able to learn from experiences more effectively. It would also have helped them form stronger social bonds and cooperate better in group activities like hunting. It seems that once the seed of conscious awareness was planted, it grew rapidly by natural selection. Rather than "survival of the fittest", it was more "survival of the most consciously aware"!

When I think about the evolution of conscious awareness, my mind boggles. Even thinking about its emergence in young children is hard to comprehend. Being consciously aware may feel normal, but it's actually something extraordinary. It's what makes us who we are and what allows us to marvel at the natural world in a way no other animal can.

The Birth of "I" and "Me"

And did you know that being consciously aware only begins to tell the story of the human condition? You are more than an animal that's aware of its own awareness. There's something else that emerges from conscious awareness that makes us even more human. Ask yourself *who* is reading this book.

I'd be surprised if your response was, "My brain". You're more likely to say, "I am". "I" is the word we use to describe our brain's awareness of its own awareness. Rather than saying, "This brain is aware that this brain is reading", we simply say, "I am reading". We effectively take our brains out of the equation altogether. "I" is a logical shortcut as soon as conscious awareness is present. While I have written "I" here as a word, it might be best thought of as a feeling or a *sense* of "I". It's a feeling that there's "something" aware of awareness, and it's a feeling that transcends language. It's what our early ancestors would have felt and what you and I first experienced in early infancy.

To be consciously aware is to have an "I". The "I" represents the observer of whatever is observed. The "I" hears sounds and sees sights. It's present as soon as we open our eyes in the morning and is the perceiver of all we perceive. Animals do not have an "I" because their brains are not aware of themselves. The "I" is, therefore, a uniquely human phenomenon which represents the lived experience of conscious awareness.

As babies become consciously aware, they recognize that their bodies belong to them. They have fingers and toes they can move. When they pick something up, they feel its weight in their hands. Before long, they realize that this "me" has a name and other people's "mes" have names too.

As the feeling of "me" strengthens, the distinction between the observer and the observed begins to fade. If my body's "Tom", it's logical that the thing aware of "Tom" and the thing controlling "Tom" is also "Tom"! An all-inclusive "sense of

Tom" emerges, and it is this that many people think of as "self-awareness".

For young children, this "self" that they're aware of simply represents their bodies. This is the self in its most basic form where it is analogous to the physical "me". Here, self-awareness refers to the child's conscious recognition that their body is their own.

The emergence of conscious awareness and self-awareness during infancy is almost impossible for us to fully grasp because we can't remember it. When I reflect on my childhood, I find myself asking the question, "When was Tom actually born?" Most of us would assume that "Tom" existed from birth or even before birth, and the only thing that changed was my awareness that I *am* Tom. The idea that Tom was already "there" is easier for most of us to comprehend than the idea that Tom didn't exist at all until a certain degree of conscious awareness. However, without conscious awareness, "Tom" was only an idea in the minds of others. "I" was actually born some months after birth and "Tom" arrived sometime after that!

Closing Thoughts

The name *homo sapien* means "wise human" in Latin. While we are certainly intelligent, it is not this quality that distinguishes us from other species. What makes us human is our unique conscious awareness and our ability to be self-aware. This miraculous capability is something no other animal can demonstrate, at least nowhere near to the extent that we do. If the human condition and the psychological pain associated with it are exclusively human, it stands to reason that there must be something about being self-aware that causes us to suffer in the manner that we do.

Knowing this allows us to make our first deduction:

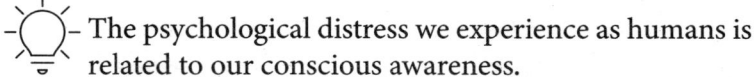 – The psychological distress we experience as humans is related to our conscious awareness.

For us to understand what is inherently painful about being self-aware, we must next make sense of what this self really is and the relationship which exists between the "I" and the "me". We must, therefore, delve deeper into the mysterious and metaphysical realms of the mind. It is here where we will find our answers.

REFLECTION

Sometimes when I'm out walking I see deer. Whenever I do, I stop and stay as still as possible. Often, the deer does the same. If I'm lucky, we share a few seconds together before its instinct to flee takes over. For a fleeting moment, our lives intersect – two animals aware of each other's presence. It doesn't know who I am. It has no understanding of the complexities of my life or the struggles I might be facing. It knows nothing about me. In fact, it knows nothing about itself – or anything else, for that matter. It sees me, but it's unaware that it's seeing me. It can smell my scent on the breeze but it's unaware it's smelling me. Its heart pounds but it's not aware that it's afraid. When the deer turns to flee, it runs not because it's frightened. It simply runs because it runs.

"The brain is wider than the sky."

Emily Dickinson

MAKING SENSE
OF THE SELF

Have you been in a group situation when you were asked to tell everyone a bit about yourself? It's a scenario that fills most of us with dread. Speaking in front of an audience is bad enough but speaking about ourselves feels even worse. Often in these situations a coordinator picks on people one by one to talk. If you're lucky, you're not chosen first because the person who starts has no reference point and must make a calculated guess as to what and how much to reveal.

Usually, people take a safe approach, providing information such as their age, where they're from and what they do for a living. If the coordinator accepts these answers, the rest of the group lets out a collective internal sigh of relief, knowing that they can follow this same framework. However, sometimes, the first person goes rogue. Rather than keeping to the standard approach, they may begin by listing fun facts about themselves, or worse, lead with "My friends would say that I'm…". Panic ripples through the room as everyone collectively thinks, "There is nothing interesting about me or my life". As for what friends say about us – do we list positive qualities and risk coming across as egotistical or do we err on the side of modesty and risk eliciting a toe-curling sympathetic "aww" from the group?

I've been in more than my fair share of such situations. I recall one forced team-building event where the coordinator suddenly pointed straight at me and said, "Who are you?"

"Er... I am... Tom."

"That's your name. Who *is* Tom?"

I hesitated. Looked around nervously.

I played it safe. This was no time to be creative. I could already sense the suspicious faces of those around me, ready to denounce me if I chose the wrong response.

"I'm 28... work as a doctor... live in London".

"I didn't ask *what* you are, I asked *who* you are!"

By this point, my cheeks were flushed red, sweat dripped down my back and I had vowed never to return to this class.

"My friends would probably say I'm..."

"I don't care what your friends would say! What would *you* say?"

After a few minutes of gut-wrenching awkwardness, the coordinator moved on to another victim, who reassuringly was as perplexed and embarrassed as me.

Few of us find "who are you?" an easy question to answer, even if we're not put on the spot and humiliated! It's a question that asks us to look directly at the self – our self. Something we're intimately familiar with, yet find incredibly difficult to define. I am "myself" and you are "yourself". But what is this self that we both take ownership of?

You are What You are

We have seen how the observing "I" of conscious awareness emerges in our infancy and recognizes our existence. We described this as "self-awareness". It is an apt description since we're describing our conscious awareness of our self.

Early self-awareness is an awareness of the first of many "self-elements". The *physical body* that an infant first becomes aware of is one of a number of self-elements that make up "what we are". Since these self-elements are found outside of our minds, they can also be considered aspects of the external self.

It is important to emphasize at this point that while I use the term "what we are" when describing these self-elements, it's purely descriptive, and I'm at no point suggesting that any of these things are truly representative of you as a person, nor am I assigning any value to them. For now, we are simply categorizing the various self-elements that most people can relate to. Some will feel more relevant to you than others. This is to be expected, and at this stage, it's helpful to recognize which self-elements resonate with you the most. How we relate to these different aspects of the self significantly shapes our experience.

Let's take a look at these external self-elements:

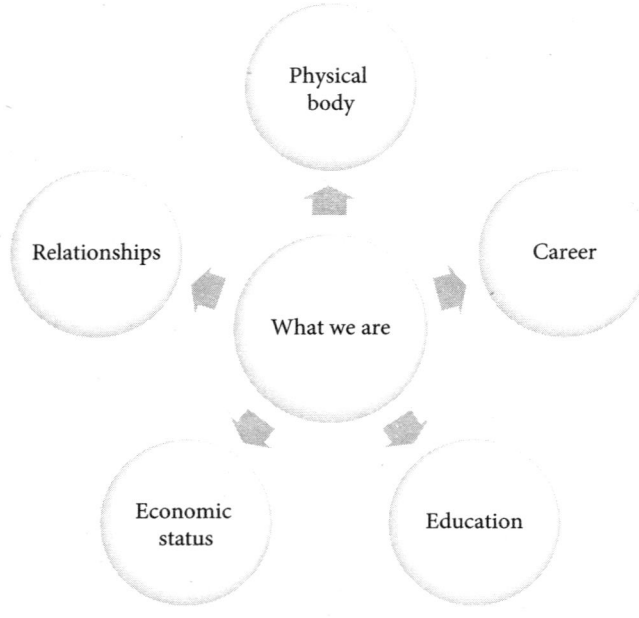

Each of these five self-elements contains within them various sub-elements. The *physical body* includes our physical form and the various aspects of our appearance, like height, weight and other physical attributes. It also encompasses our age, fitness and physical health.

Career refers to our occupation, employment status, job title and role. It tends to be closely associated with *education* and *economic status*. Our *education* includes where we went to school, our academic achievements and qualifications, while our *economic status* incorporates our financial status, income, material possessions and property ownership.

Finally, we have *relationships*. This includes being a parent, partner, friend, sibling, colleague and any other social role we hold.

You are Who You are

The five external self-elements are often easily recognizable in ourselves and others. Like all aspects of the self, they can be observed and discussed objectively. While these self-elements provide us with some information about someone, describing ourselves purely as "what we are" would undoubtedly fail to do us justice.

Imagine one of your friends wants to introduce you to somebody they know. It is someone they know well but you've never met them. Your friend says that you've got loads in common and you'd hit it off. Curious, you ask your friend what this person is like. They tell you that they're a teacher and studied history at university. They say this person is single and attractive. If you were single yourself, you might find your curiosity piqued! So far, so good.

"But what are they like, as a *person*?"

This is the dealbreaker. Your friend has described a little about *what* this person is, but you now want to know *who* this person is. Are they nice? Do they believe erroneously that the Earth is flat? These are things that you would probably want to know about beforehand!

These aspects of a person are not found in the external self. They're not part of "what we are" but rather "who we are". They are the internal self, which is also made up of various self-elements. While I refer to them as internal, it doesn't mean they're necessarily hidden or unrecognizable to others. They remain objective in nature and, sometimes, just as evident externally in how they're expressed as elements of "what we are" – often more so! I describe them as internal because these self-elements tend to arise from inside our minds.

Here they are:

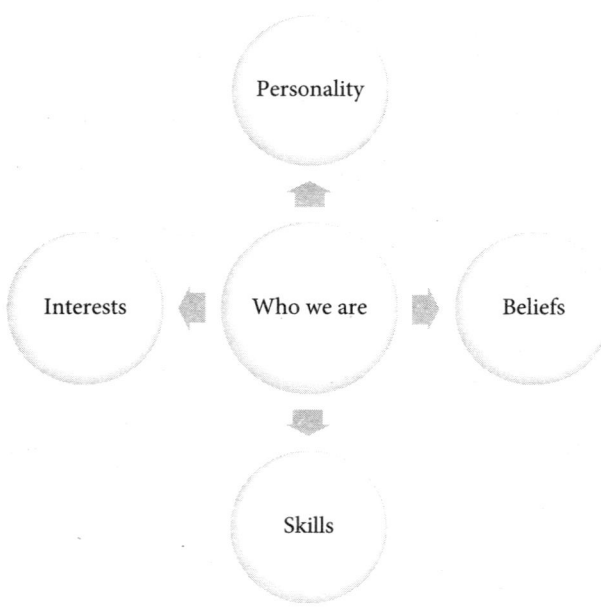

Personality refers to our character and is broken down by psychologists into five sub-categories[1]:

1. Openness: our willingness to embrace new experiences, ideas and ways of thinking.
2. Conscientiousness: how organized, responsible and dependable we are.
3. Extraversion: how sociable and assertive we are.
4. Agreeableness: our inclination towards cooperation, empathy and kindness (indicating our level of warmth, compassion and consideration for others).
5. Neuroticism: our tendency to experience emotions like anxiety, sadness and anger.

These five character traits are considered as scales. For example, rather than somebody being conscientious or not, we think of the extent to which a person is conscientious. While we may have our opinions as to how desirable or undesirable these aspects of *personality* are, and indeed to what degree somebody expresses them, they should be considered neutral characteristics, neither inherently good nor bad. *Personality* is an aspect of the self that's most affected by subjectivity and individual interpretation.

Alongside this self-element, we have our *beliefs*, *skills* and *interests*. Our *beliefs* incorporate our values and opinions, including religious or spiritual, political ideologies, moral values and personal philosophies. *Skills* refer to our natural talents like musical or athletic flair as well as those we have learnt through experience or training. They are commonly linked to our *interests*. These represent our passions, hobbies and things we enjoy in our free time.

Overall, our *personality*, *beliefs*, *skills* and *interests* define our internal self. These aspects of "who we are" come together with the elements of "what we are" to produce what I refer to as the self. A single, objective entity comprising internal and external self-elements.

The Interconnected Self

While I have listed the various self-elements as separate components of the self, it is important to recognize that no self-element exists in isolation.

For example, let's look at *career*.

Career choices are influenced by personal values (*beliefs*) and the things we enjoy (*interests*). Our work can help us network professionally and may impact our social roles (*relationships*). Our jobs also largely determine our finances and ability to buy things (*economic status*). How we perform in our careers is affected by how we react to tasks and challenges that arise at work and this is heavily influenced by our character traits (*personality*). And, of course, our ability to perform work-related tasks often depends on us needing to learn specific technical and non-technical competencies (*skills*).

Each self-element is directly or indirectly connected to all the others. This means that there's no separation between our internal and external selves. The self exists as a complex web of interconnected self-elements. This explains why we often find it challenging to tell people about ourselves. To understand one self-element, it is necessary to appreciate its place alongside the rest.

The Dynamic Self

Not only are self-elements interconnected but they're also in constant flux. This means that the self is more like a living organism, its form forever shifting as individual self-elements change and the relationships between them evolve. Change affecting one self-element invariably leads to change in another. For example, becoming a parent may influence your choice of career. It may also change your values and affect your relationships with friends. You may discover new hobbies and your financial situation may be impacted.

Self-elements may change suddenly and drastically or gradually and subtly. The speed and degree of change will affect how much this change is felt across other aspects of the self. This change may happen spontaneously from within a self-element or in response to something outside of the self entirely. To complicate matters further, not only is every individual self-element interconnected, but through our relationships with other people, our selves are intertwined with the selves of others! Your self is, therefore, inseparable from the world around you and shaped by it, much like the growth of a tree is influenced by the seasons.

Change is Variable

Although every self-element changes, certain self-elements are more volatile than others. Typically, internal self-elements are more fixed than external ones that tend to be more exposed to outside influences and therefore more vulnerable to change.

Personality is an aspect of the self that we see as relatively static because we can trace many aspects of our personality back to childhood. Until relatively recently, the common view among many psychologists and psychiatrists was that personality is unchanging. Even today, many mental health professionals see personality as something set in stone. This has meant some regard so-called "personality disorders", such as borderline personality disorder (BPD), as incurable problems.

I find the notion that such disorders (if they're disorders at all) are untreatable, both illogical and unhelpful in supporting people who may be struggling. Fortunately, how people see personality and personality disorders is changing, supported by research by Srivastava et al., (2003) which shows that personality evolves over time[2]. These changes may not be as sudden or as obvious as perhaps a job loss, but they're nevertheless happening.

This kind of gradual change is also seen in our *beliefs*. While they can change quickly with sudden insights and epiphanies, they usually develop slowly in response to cultural and societal changes as well as through continuous life experiences.

From Self to Self-Perception

It is important to remember that the self we are describing is exclusively human because it is dependent on conscious awareness. Without the observing "I", the self would not exist. And yet, despite the self's reliance on the observing "I", this "I" remains an impartial witness. It doesn't judge what it sees and cannot exert any influence. It is a neutral spectator that simply represents conscious awareness. If I were to ask you, "How do you feel about yourself?" it would be your observing "I" that would be aware of the question. It would also be aware of the answer but it wouldn't be responsible for formulating the response!

But if it's not the "I" that decides how I feel about myself, then *who* is it? As weird as it sounds, the answer's "nobody". Your feelings about yourself, or "self-perception", emerge into your conscious awareness from the interplay between your self and unconscious parts of your brain.

Here, your *beliefs* self-element plays a pivotal role. This is because among your many beliefs, you'll have specific beliefs about each of your self-elements. For example, you may believe that introversion is a negative personality trait or that your career can only be successful if you're earning a specific wage.

All your beliefs about your self-elements create a blueprint against which your brain assesses them. In other words, your brain evaluates each self-element and decides whether it is good or bad according to a standard created from your beliefs. The result of this assessment then manifests in your conscious awareness as self-perception.

To see how this works, I'd like to share an experience I had when I was at school. I was teased for having red hair. For a few years, I was subjected to daily comments about how unattractive it was to have my hair colour. For the first few months, I was confused, as it had never been an issue in primary school and my family had always spoken about it as if it were a positive thing. However, over time I started to feel more insecure about it. I learnt that it was undesirable and I began to feel different to everybody else. Before long, my self-esteem was non-existent and I found myself increasingly anxious. A part of me knew how irrational it was but I couldn't help but feel like I didn't belong.

You might notice two self-elements highlighted here – my *physical body* (in this case, my hair) and my *beliefs*. The ongoing teasing I experienced gradually changed my core beliefs about what I thought it meant to be attractive. As these beliefs deepened, my brain began to evaluate my physical body self-element more negatively. As I became aware of the disparity between what my self-element was and what it "should" be, my self-perception deteriorated with worsening self-esteem.

This is an oversimplification of what happens when a child is bullied. Bullying doesn't just impact a couple of self-elements. It can affect a child's ability to make friends (*relationships*), their participation in leisure activities (*interests*) and their schoolwork (*education*). These then influence how the child's self is evaluated, damaging self-perception even further.

While this example highlights the impact of negative self-perception, it's important to bear in mind that self-elements can also be evaluated positively, giving rise to positive self-perception. Right now, you'll have a general feeling about yourself as well as specific feelings about individual self-elements. Your self-perception, just like your self, will continuously evolve as self-elements change. Due to the significant role that your beliefs play in shaping your self-perception, changes here can have a huge knock-on effect on how multiple self-elements are perceived for better or worse.

Who Am I?

With the revelation that *you* are not actively responsible for determining how you feel about yourself, there are even deeper, philosophical questions that must be asked. Ones which expose a paradox at the very heart of our human experience.

Who is consciously aware? Who does this self belong to? Who feels positively or negatively about themselves? Let's ask this in a different way, using me as an example. If Tom is *not* conscious awareness itself, and Tom is *not* the self or the brain's assessment of the self, then who or what the **** is Tom?!

Just like nobody decides how you feel about yourself, there's seemingly nobody to feel anything towards. What I call "Tom" is nothing more than a fictional character that my brain has created to make sense of what's happening.

Rather than seeing conscious awareness, the self, and self-perception as "owner-less" phenomena of the brain, we naturally assume these things belong to our fictional character (in my case, Tom). It is Tom who's self-aware and it's Tom who feels good or bad about himself.

From now on, when I refer to this fictional character, I will refer to it as our "Person". It is through the creation of this Person that our brains make sense of the total mystery which is conscious awareness. While our Person may be fictional, this does not mean that it doesn't exist. It's simply that what is there is not what we imagine it to be. A photo is still a real photo, even if it's not actually the person themselves!

Just like a photo of me is a projection of an image onto a reel of film, my self and self-perception are also projected onto the canvas of conscious awareness to create the Person I know to be Tom. This Person is a mirage created in the mind's eye. There is actually no "thinker of a thought" or "feeler of an emotion". There's no perceiver of the self. The self is simply perceived by the brain. This perception is then assigned to our Person in our brain's attempt to rationalize its own self-awareness.

Closing Thoughts

Confused?! You may be comforted to know that we all are! Understanding the self and our relationship with it takes us from the physical to the metaphysical and seemingly even beyond that. The complexities of our minds are beyond anything any of us can comprehend. We shouldn't be surprised if we're confused! As soon as our brains became aware of themselves, Pandora's Box was well and truly opened. It's a miracle that being human feels as normal as it does!

So, are you ready for our second deduction?

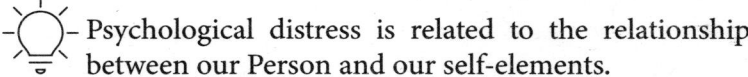 Psychological distress is related to the relationship between our Person and our self-elements.

But what is it about this relationship that hurts so much? To answer this question, we need to understand how our minds and brains come into conflict.

REFLECTION

I've spent a great deal of my life wondering who I am. When my life got tough, I lost sight of who I was and became transfixed with the Person I wanted to be and how my life *should* look. My brain held within it a blueprint which bore no resemblance to the imperfect self that it saw. Faced with such a problem, I did what most people would do and tried to better myself in any way that I could. But no matter what I tried, I couldn't make it look the way I wanted it to look. There was nothing I could do to fix it. Gradually, as my life fell apart, I began to realize there was something I had overlooked. My self wasn't the problem. I'd been using the wrong blueprint. And perhaps no blueprint was needed at all.

"Knowing yourself is the beginning of all wisdom."

Aristotle

THE SELF: A GATEWAY TO PSYCHOLOGICAL PAIN

What do you think of when I use the term "psychological pain"? What memories come to mind? What feelings do you associate with these words?

I think about fear and recall how it feels to be anxious. I remember the feeling of butterflies in my stomach and my heart thumping in my chest. I recall times when I felt intense feelings of sorrow. I remember what it's like to be tearful and that feeling of emptiness in my body.

We all experience a wide range of emotions, but if there were two words that perhaps best encapsulate them, they would probably be fear and sadness. Even strong emotions like anger and guilt can usually be traced to an underlying fear or sorrow. Fear and sadness are feelings everyone can relate to. But while they feel human, we have already seen that complex emotional states such as these are by no means exclusively ours. We can observe behaviours indicative of fear and sadness right across the animal kingdom.

However, as people, we experience these complex emotional states differently from other animals. We suffer in a human way. Our fear is felt as worry, stress and anxiety.

Our sadness may be experienced as shame, guilt and hopelessness. Something about the human condition elevates and complicates these emotional states. For us to understand what that is, we must trace our psychological pain back to its biological beginnings. From there, we can see why we have come to suffer like we do today.

The Origins of Pain

From a biological perspective, fear and sadness can be defined as an interplay between key chemicals: adrenaline, cortisol, serotonin, dopamine and noradrenaline. These chemicals likely evolved hundreds of millions of years ago when they played basic functions, helping simple multicellular organisms adapt to their environments. Initially, they would have been involved in processes like regulating energy, responding to environmental stressors and basic movement. As organisms became increasingly complex, the chemicals would have assumed more sophisticated roles supporting various processes. In time, whole systems developed around these chemicals, forming intricate networks within the brain and body. Today, these chemicals and systems are found throughout the animal kingdom, highlighting their ancient evolutionary roots and their universal importance in sustaining life.

Of all the systems, the fear response system has been the most studied. When an animal detects a threat, "stress chemicals", including adrenaline, are released, and these travel in the bloodstream, having effects all over the body. Adrenaline increases the heart rate, promotes heat loss and diverts blood to the muscles. Other chemicals, such as cortisol, help to mobilize energy reserves. They increase physical endurance and prepare the animal for fight or flight. These chemicals have effects not only on the body but also on the brain. They make the animal more alert, enhance its senses and trigger an instinctive urge to escape to safety. The fear response system is a finely tuned, built-in security system that prepares an animal for potential danger, giving it the best possible chance to survive.

While this system evolved purely to respond to threats, other systems arose to reinforce behaviours that would support survival over the medium to long term. These included behaviours involved in finding food and reproduction. It's here that dopamine, the brain's feel-good chemical, deserves a mention. Dopamine plays a central role in our reward system, where it helps to ensure that crucial activities like eating and mating are not only carried out but actively enjoyed. It's the system responsible for the so-called dopamine hit when we demolish a tub of ice cream.

Although a clear correlation exists between increased dopamine and feeling good, the relationship between dopamine and feeling sad is more complicated. Sadness is a complex emotional state that involves multiple chemical systems and areas of the brain. It is generally seen in more evolved animals, mostly mammals, and correlates with advanced behaviours like social bonding. Where fear appears to be a more primitive and widely experienced state, sadness emerges from the interplay between various chemicals. This is also true of anxiety, which is much more than the ongoing activation of the fear response system. In fact, there's actually a significant crossover between the biochemical basis of sadness and anxiety, which points to their complex and interconnected nature. For example, the chemical serotonin acts as a mood regulator, influencing how contented we feel and our stress levels.

But none of the chemicals found in our brains are exclusively human. As complicated as the human brain is, it's not novel biochemically. The same chemicals and pathways exist in most animals and serve similar and often identical functions. While science can tell us what might be going on from a physiological perspective, science cannot tell us why our experience of psychological pain is unlike anything else seen in nature despite being from the same building blocks. We are more than the sum of our biological parts and are again left asking the same question. If such a similarity exists between humans and animals, what is it about the human condition that makes our experience so unique?

Biology Meets Awareness

As discussed, the biological systems described above are activated when an animal's needs are not being met or when they're under threat. When their brain detects an essential need is unmet, the animal instinctively responds with behaviours that hopefully resolve the issue. Similarly, if its fight or flight response is activated, it will instinctively behave in ways that will increase its odds of survival.

These instinctive behavioural responses seen in animals occur without conscious awareness. When an animal's body detects it's dehydrated, the animal seeks water without thinking, "I am thirsty and I need water". Similarly, if a pack animal is separated from the herd, at no point does it think, "I am alone". However, its brain automatically interprets the situation and encourages it to rejoin the herd.

But as we already know thanks to conscious awareness, our experience is very different from other animals. We *know* when we're thirsty and we *know* when we're in danger. Not only do we receive the physiological boosts to fight strongly or flee quickly, we don't rely solely on instinct. We can use intelligence to avoid threatening situations. Conscious awareness means we can also seek out things to meet our physical needs more shrewdly. An awareness of pleasure provides us with added motivation to engage in behaviours that are in our best interests.

Conscious awareness combined with complex biological systems created a winning evolutionary formula, allowing our species to flourish and dominate the planet. The benefit gained in relation to physical needs and the fear response likely provided the evolutionary pressure needed for the rapid expansion of conscious awareness in humans.

An Awareness of Pain

However, this evolutionary gift did not come for free, as we can see by how conscious awareness affects our experience of fear. An awareness of fear means we *feel* fear. We're aware of our fast heart rate. We feel our clammy palms. We notice a growing sickness in our stomachs. Fear feels uncomfortable and we don't like it.

And guess what? The fact that it's unpleasant is another evolutionary trick. Our displeasure makes us even more likely to avoid threats. Therefore it is highly likely that with our emerging conscious awareness, our fear response evolved to become uncomfortable! And if that is not enough, our fear response was also designed to be very sensitive. After all, it's safer to respond to something that's not threatening rather than risk not reacting to a genuine danger. This can be observed by how we might react when somebody pops up from our periphery and makes us jump. Our hearts will race and our muscles might tense before we have time to fully process whether or not we are in a threatening situation. Not only did our fear response evolve to cause us discomfort, but it also evolved to have an "itchy trigger finger".

Our awareness of fear gives rise to the first level of suffering unique to our experience as people. It's a discomfort caused directly by our awareness of our biological systems and a form of suffering evolution probably actively encouraged. After all, it's more important for an organism to survive than to feel comfortable!

It's a similar picture when it comes to our physical needs. When our needs are unmet and our biological systems respond, we know what's happening. This means we feel the discomfort related to unmet physical needs. Again, this discomfort acts as a stick, encouraging us to change our behaviours to satisfy unmet needs. For example, hunger is an unpleasant feeling that motivates us to eat food. The dopamine hit we gain from eating is the "carrot" that helps to encourage us to avoid being hungry in future.

Not only are we consciously aware of our physical needs being unmet but we're also consciously aware of what might happen if they're not met. This means that we interpret unmet physical needs as indirect threats. When a dog's hungry, it doesn't think, "If I don't eat, I might get sick or starve". Hunger doesn't make the dog afraid. However, for us, conscious awareness means that we experience pain from the unmet need now and pain from our projection of what it might mean for us moving forward. This further intensifies the suffering we experience around unmet physical needs. It also suggests one of the reasons why the crossover exists between the various chemicals related to anxiety and sadness.

This first level of human suffering is only the tip of the iceberg. Conscious awareness has plenty more tricks up its sleeve. These can be revealed when we consider what happens during a panic attack.

Seeing is Believing

A panic attack starts when the brain detects what it believes to be a threat. It reacts by triggering the fear response, releasing stress chemicals such as adrenaline and cortisol into the bloodstream. This primes the body and mind for action and makes us feel the sensations we associate with fear, like a racing heart and an increased breathing rate.

At this point, the fear response is in full flow, and everything is happening as it should. However in a panic attack, fear effectively turns on itself. The person interprets the uncomfortable physical sensations as a sign that something's wrong or that something terrible might be about to happen. This makes the individual feel even more afraid as the threat level grows. This activates the fear response even more, leading to more stress chemicals flooding the body. This results in even more discomfort, confirming the unfortunate person's predictions of impending catastrophe. With their worst fears seemingly coming true, panic sets in.

Panic attacks are therefore a cycle of worsening physical discomfort and increasing levels of fear. They are extremely common and highlight the power of the fight and flight response to overwhelm the consciously aware brain.

Panic attacks also highlight something else about our experience of fear. They show the fear response can be triggered by actual and *perceived* threats. In a panic attack, the person's conscious awareness of a rapid heart rate or a feeling of discomfort in the chest is misinterpreted as a sign that something terrible's about to happen such as a heart attack, despite no actual threat being present. The individual perceives there to be one, which is enough to trigger the fear response. In other words, the conscious mind can trigger the unconscious fear response even in the absence of genuine danger.

This ability to consciously provoke the fear response likely evolved as a failsafe mechanism to ensure our ancestors could still respond with maximum effectiveness to a threat that their unconscious brain may have missed. For example, imagine a hunter walking through a thick forest in a region known to be inhabited by dangerous tribes. Perhaps they recognize some faint tracks on the ground or broken sticks that may indicate danger. These subtle, ambiguous signs of threat may only have been detected by conscious recognition using higher cognitive functions. The hunter's ability to detect this threat early might be critical to avoiding a dangerous encounter. However, what if these tracks and broken sticks were not created by a dangerous tribe? What if they were made by the very animal the hunter was looking for instead?

The hunter's misinterpretation of the situation might lead to them returning home without food. However, they would be alive, even if they were hungry. Here, we can see that evolution prioritized survival over comfort and immediate survival over longer-term needs such as food.

In a panic attack, a person's brain is trying to prioritize survival but the threat it's trying to escape from is a feature of the very response designed to help it escape! The self-perpetuating loop of fear is why panic attacks are known as panic cycles. These cycles are an intriguing and unintended consequence of conscious awareness in the context of the fear response. They demonstrate how we can consciously activate an otherwise unconscious biological mechanism and how our perception of a situation can be just as important as what is actually happening.

Physical and Metaphysical Survival

There's another feature that's often seen in panic attacks that illustrates something even more remarkable about the human condition. It can be seen in the following internal dialogue that someone may have in the build-up to a panic attack.

"It's quite cramped on this bus.

It's making me feel uncomfortable.

I hope I won't need to get off this bus in a hurry.

Getting off this bus would be almost impossible.

Imagine if I had a panic attack now! How terrible that would be.

Awful, I'd totally humiliate myself.

Uh oh, I'm starting to feel bad now."

Again, here, we can see that panic attacks can be triggered by perceived rather than actual threats. However, this example also shows us that the fear response is triggered not only by threats to the physical body but by perceived threats to our Person.

For this individual on the bus, the threat of humiliation was the key driver for the panic cycle. Fear of embarrassment is a common feature of panic attacks and is usually linked to some of the physical effects of the fear response, such as facial flushing, sweating and trembling. Someone may even interpret light-headedness as a sign they may faint. They imagine what it would be like to collapse in front of loads of people and how humiliating it would be. They might be so concerned about the thought of embarrassing themselves they don't even consider the potential physical harm that could result from falling.

The discovery that threats to our Person can activate the fear response shows us that the evolution of fear in humans crossed the boundary between biology and metaphysics. Humans evolved to keep both their bodies *and* their Persons safe. In other words, we're driven by an instinctive need to survive and a *desire* to exist beyond our physical form.

As the human species evolved to have increasing conscious awareness, it also evolved to have an increasing sense of self and a growing want to survive. This would further enhance humanity's survival odds. In time, threats to the Person became just as significant as threats to the body. When considering modern life, you may argue that many of us now value our Person much more than our physical safety. We care about our bodies because we rely on them for our brains and minds. Even those who place significant value on their bodies often only do so because they depend on them for parts of their self-image.

Human Needs

The discovery that threats to the Person can elicit the fear response gives us the first clue as to why we're vulnerable to psychological pain. But, as we know, human suffering encompasses a range of emotions which extend far beyond fear. We have seen that we suffer when our physical needs are unmet. However, human needs are not only physical. We also have psychological needs.

To call these psychological needs "needs" at all is perhaps already a contentious use of language. If our body doesn't have food or water, it will die. If our psychological needs are unmet, does our Person die? Does the mind need anything other than the brain to function? These thought-provoking questions are not straightforward to answer.

However, it's generally accepted by psychologists that we need certain things psychologically to maintain a healthy state of mind. The extent to which these psychological needs are actual or perceived is open to interpretation. It seems that the decision as to whether these needs are met or unmet depends mostly on whether somebody believes them to be met. And whether these needs are needs at all will depend on whether someone believes they are.

For example, do you *need* to have a romantic partner? Some say yes, while others say absolutely not. Even those who believe they do may find themselves in a relationship which doesn't fulfil their needs. Whether their need for a romantic partner is satisfied depends more on how they evaluate their relationship rather than whether or not they have one.

Whenever we believe that a psychological need is unmet, our brains will respond predictably, regardless of the nature of this need and we'll feel bad. This is because our brain biochemistry will change with reward chemicals being down-regulated and stress chemicals being released.

Our brains and biological systems do not distinguish between physical and psychological needs, just like they do not distinguish between threats to our Person and threats to our body. If the consciously aware mind believes there's an unmet need or a threatening situation, our brains will respond predictably to help us resolve the problem. Inherent to this response is the unpleasant experience that we feel as psychological pain.

The Nature of Psychological Needs

The psychological needs we have as humans is a topic that psychologists have studied extensively for decades. One notable figure in this research area is Abraham Maslow, who categorized what he thought were core human needs into a hierarchy known as Maslow's hierarchy of needs. In his model, Maslow arranged human needs according to their relative importance in what he described as a progression toward self-actualization. This is often presented as a pyramid with basic or fundamental human needs at the bottom and more complex needs toward the top.

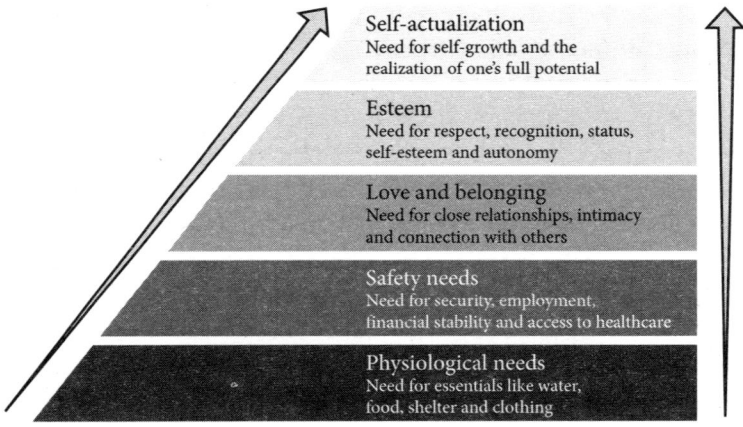

Self-actualization
Need for self-growth and the realization of one's full potential

Esteem
Need for respect, recognition, status, self-esteem and autonomy

Love and belonging
Need for close relationships, intimacy and connection with others

Safety needs
Need for security, employment, financial stability and access to healthcare

Physiological needs
Need for essentials like water, food, shelter and clothing

Maslow believed that higher needs only emerge once the more basic needs have been satisfied. Therefore, only once our physiological needs have been met do we prioritize our safety needs. These include health, financial security and social stability. Satisfying these helps us feel safe physically and emotionally. After this has been achieved, our next focus is love and belonging. This represents our need for intimate relationships and human connection. It emphasizes the importance of family and friendships. Next, Maslow identifies our needs related to esteem. This includes the need for healthy self-esteem, status and recognition. It is the need to feel good about ourselves and the desire to be accepted by others. The apex of the pyramid is self-actualization, representing what Maslow believed to be the highest level of human need. This relates to our pursuit to realize our potential and become the best versions of ourselves. We aspire to live a meaningful life and our focus is on self-growth.

Of course, Maslow's ideas are not without criticism. For example, many see this model as an oversimplification of human needs. They feel it's too rigid in its implication that some needs are beyond reach until others are fulfilled. They argue that in real life, many people pursue different levels of the hierarchy simultaneously, which contradicts the idea of linear hierarchical progression. Others highlight that the model's biased toward a Western culture, where there's greater emphasis on individuality and self-actualization. Some also feel it fails to reflect the fluidity of needs between individuals and variations across different life stages.

I agree with all of these criticisms but despite the model's limitations, Maslow's ideas serve as a fantastic framework for discussing psychological needs.

Needs and the Self

When we look at Maslow's model in the context of the self, we can see some interesting similarities between what Maslow describes as human needs and what we have discussed in relation to the self. At each level of Maslow's hierarchy, there are various internal and external self-elements related to specific needs.

For example, *relationships* help to fulfil our needs for friendship, intimacy, family and a sense of connection. Our *career* can bring us financial security, respect and status. Our *beliefs* affect our self-esteem and influence the Person we want to become.

While our model of the self is inherently non-linear and dynamic, there are enough similarities between the two to suggest that a relationship exists between the self and our psychological needs. We should regard self-elements as serving vital functions in fulfilling our psychological needs. Our self-elements are to our Persons as food, water and air are to our bodies. Our brains combine our various self-elements into a psychological solution that we use to fulfil the needs of our Person.

As we saw regarding self-perception, this solution is based largely on our beliefs about our psychological needs. Despite their clearly subjective nature, it is also clear that you and I share certain needs that transcend our personal beliefs, almost as if they were in some way hardwired.

The Origins of Psychological Needs

When it comes to psychological needs, there's a compelling argument suggesting that genetics plays an important role. This is particularly relevant when we consider needs that Maslow described as relating to "safety" and "love and belonging". The need for secure attachments and social connections have a basis in our evolutionary history, where survival depended on being part of a group. The ability of early humans to form strong bonds would have been crucial in their ability to hunt, live together safely, reproduce and successfully raise families.

Of course, these behaviours are also important in other animals, as we saw when we discussed wolves earlier in the book. In animals, these behaviours are primarily instinctive, which means they must have a genetic basis. This is because instincts are inherited traits that are encoded in an animal's DNA, ensuring that these behaviours are passed down from generation to generation without the need for learning. This can be seen, for example, in how a bird instinctively knows how to build a nest or when turtles naturally head towards the ocean immediately after hatching on the beach. This genetic programming is shared among many species, including human beings, where it's likely to be even more advanced than in other animals.

However, behaviour, especially in humans, is shaped by experience. Our instincts are influenced by our upbringing, life events, culture and society. These factors can significantly impact our beliefs regarding what needs are important and what we need in order for them to be fulfilled. For example, the needs for "esteem" and "self-actualization" might manifest differently across cultures. In societies which emphasize individuality, a person may be more likely to value personal achievement and independence. In contrast, societies that place a greater emphasis on family and community may value relationships and social connections more than personal accolades and individual accomplishments.

We should also consider that new psychological needs may emerge over the course of a person's lifetime depending on life events and new perspectives. For example, a particularly impactful or transformative romantic relationship may change what someone feels they need from future relationships.

While many of our psychological needs undoubtedly have a genetic basis, how each of us relates to them and experiences them is heavily influenced by our lived experience.

Who Has Needs?

When we speak about psychological needs, it is important to keep in mind that *who* it is that has these needs isn't necessarily as obvious as it might seem. Just like there is "nobody" responsible for our self-perception and "nobody" that self-perceives, there is also "nobody" that these psychological needs belong to. Just like our self and self-perception are projected by our brains onto our Person, our brains also assign these psychological needs to our Person.

In my case, "Tom" has the need for security. It is Tom who needs love and belonging. The "I" of conscious awareness is simply aware of my Person's, Tom's, needs. When we say, "*I* need to feel loved", this assumes the seat of conscious awareness is within our Person itself rather than emerging from the brain's self-awareness.

It is perhaps too strong to argue that psychological needs don't exist at all, but there is a strong argument to suggest they don't exist in the way that most psychologists believe they do.

The Painful Self

Regardless of exactly *how* or *why* our psychological needs arise and, indeed, *who* they actually belong to(!), each of us will recognize self-elements that serve to fulfil critical needs. It is our self-elements' role in meeting our needs that holds the secret as to why the human condition is inherently painful. This is because relying on the self to fulfil our critical needs is like relying on a friend who lets you down at every available opportunity and in every possible way!

The problem with self-elements is that they're constantly changing. This is because they naturally evolve over time and are also extremely vulnerable to changes affecting other interconnected self-elements and changes occurring outside of the self entirely. This leaves us in a precarious position since change, which is unavoidable, invariably leads to our psychological needs being unmet sooner or later.

The threat of change makes us afraid. When changes happen, we suffer loss. The pain experienced by changes to one self-element is exacerbated by pain caused by subsequent changes to others. Threats to self-elements may arise suddenly and pass quickly or persist as ongoing risks.

This can lead to chronic stress that destabilizes the entire self. Sometimes, multiple threats emerge simultaneously, undermining multiple self-elements at the same time. It's messy, complicated and painful.

When I was struggling as a junior doctor, I experienced extremely high levels of anxiety. I was incredibly fearful of failing in some way and not making it. I put a huge amount of pressure on myself and it took everything I had just to make it through each day. Every mistake I made felt catastrophic and whenever my medical bleeper went off, I was filled with dread. The worse things got, the more my life shrunk. I was unable to sustain relationships, I lost friends, I stopped playing sports and my health deteriorated. Eventually, things got so bad that I had to leave my medical career altogether. Immediately, the anxiety I'd felt was replaced by a deep sense of loss and a gaping hole in my self.

My career fulfilled multiple critical needs for me. It gave me meaning, status, respect, self-esteem and the opportunity to connect with others. In fact, I was reliant on being a doctor for pretty much everything I cared about! It's no wonder that "losing it all" left a pretty big gap!

Closing Thoughts

The psychological pain we experience as humans can be traced back to the same biological systems present across the animal kingdom. With conscious awareness, we're aware of the discomfort caused by these systems. It's this discomfort that gives rise to the first level of human suffering. However, with conscious awareness comes the self, and it's the interactions between our self and our biological systems that produce the second level of human suffering. This is the fear and loss we experience due to real or perceived threats against our self-elements that our brains so haplessly cling to fulfil our (Person's) psychological needs.

This gives us our third deduction.

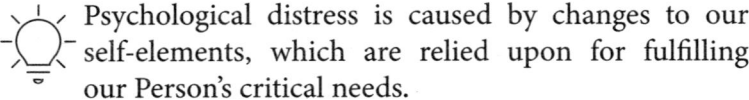 Psychological distress is caused by changes to our self-elements, which are relied upon for fulfilling our Person's critical needs.

While this chapter examines psychological pain, it's worth remembering that being human is also synonymous with *positive* human experiences. Conscious awareness means we feel pleasure in a way that animals cannot. We can experience joy that lasts beyond a single moment. We can look back on our lives and experience gratitude. We can look ahead and see hope. We can feel deep calm when we're able to escape acute stress and anxiety. These aspects of the human condition are equally valid and arguably more important. Soon, we will focus on how to make this our reality.

But first, we must take the "problem" to its natural conclusion. It's time to see why we chase the very things that are destined to cause us pain. It's time to see how we become *self-obsessed*.

REFLECTION

In 2018 I walked 2000 kilometres from Canterbury to Rome following an ancient path called the Via Francigena. It took three months. People often ask why I did it. Was it for the love of walking? Was it to explore rural France, Switzerland and Italy?

I did it because I could and I needed to. It's perhaps best understood by what somebody told me just before I started my journey. They said:

"Tom, you carry a burden that is no
longer yours to carry. It's time to let it go."
What was the burden? Who was it that couldn't let go?

*"We are what we think.
All that we are arises
with our thoughts.
With our thoughts,
we make the world."*

Buddha

FINDING PAIN IN WHAT WE VALUE THE MOST

Have you ever wondered why the same issue can affect two people in different ways? How one person may lose a parent and cope relatively well, while another may suffer from intense grief that may take years to recover from. How someone may embrace retirement with open arms, while someone else may suffer from a deep emptiness and loss of meaning in their lives. None of us *want* to suffer, yet for many of us the extent to which we do gives the impression that we might.

So, what is it that determines the degree of pain we experience? Why do certain self-elements hurt us so much more than others? Let's find out!

That Really Hurts

When self-elements change, we suffer. Whether this change is real or imagined matters little. As long as our brains conclude that one of our psychological needs is no longer being met, suffering is inevitable. The threat of this change causes us anxiety, regardless of whether this change ever happens.

However, to blame self-elements for our suffering is like blaming food for making us eat or wine for making us drink. Food and wine are innocent parties but it feels better to blame them when we eat or drink too much than to blame ourselves! Food and drink are not responsible for our greed, just like individual self-elements are not responsible for our pain.

Imagine two people who are passionate mountain bikers. Both spend as much free time as they can on their bikes, finding new trails. They are both members of mountain biker groups and spend a large proportion of their incomes on bikes and new gear. Supposing both suffer unfortunate long-term injuries that prevent them from cycling for the foreseeable future. One biker, although incredibly disappointed, sees their injury layoff as an opportunity to spend more time with friends and family. However, the other biker experiences a profound sense of loss that feels impossible to shift. Unable to do what they love makes their life feel empty and the prospect of never biking again makes them fearful for the future.

In this example, both individuals suffered a sudden change affecting their *physical body* self-element, which had an immediate knock-on effect on their *interests* self-element. They were equally passionate about their hobby, yet the two bikers felt the impact of this change very differently. This is because for one of them mountain biking was a core aspect of their *identity*.

Identity

Within the self, there are self-elements that mean more to us than others. This is based on our beliefs regarding our psychological needs and how much we see certain self-elements as being important to fulfil them. Those self-elements that we see as particularly significant constitute our identity. Our identity lies at the core of the self. It is made up of self-elements that resonate most with us. They are often linked to our values and purpose in life.

While every self-element that makes up our identity matters to us, not every self-element we care about forms part of our identity. We can value things without seeing them as fulfilling a core psychological need, especially if we have something else that we identify with that does.

For example, someone may believe that to feel safe, they need financial security. They may think this can be achieved through a job or having a partner with a stable career. If they were single, they may find themselves identifying more with their work, whereas if they had a partner, they might find that their work is a less critical aspect of their identity. Of course, if their relationship ends, then this may change.

Identity is typically made up of a mixture of internal and external self-elements. It can sometimes seem fixed, but this is likely only because it includes our *personalities* and *beliefs* that tend to change slowly. Any aspect of the self can become a central component of our identity. For the mountain biker it was one of their *interests* and for me, when I was desperately clinging to my job as a doctor, it was my *career*. For others, it might be *relationships* or their *physical bodies*, often in the context of their physical appearance.

The Vulnerability of Identity

The degree to which we *identify* with our self-elements ultimately determines how much we suffer when a self-element changes. If we identify a lot, we will suffer a lot. If we identify with many self-elements, we will suffer often. Our overall vulnerability to psychological pain is determined by the *extent* to which we identify with our self-elements and the *number* of self-elements we identify with.

Someone who identifies with relatively few self-elements may still suffer intensely if only one changes because they identify with it strongly. Conversely, someone who identifies with many self-elements but to a much lesser degree may suffer more often but less acutely. Suffering is inevitable because every self-element is subject to change. The struggle to resist this change creates stress and anxiety, the result of this change is sadness and loss. The things we value most tend to be associated with the most pain, not because of what they are but because of how we identify with them.

Our tendency to identify with the self is *self-obsession*. A literal obsession with the self – made up of the self-elements. We are all self-obsessed to a greater or lesser degree. Self-obsession is *the* problem at the heart of the human condition. It is self-obsession that fills our lives with fear and sadness and it is self-obsession that detracts from the beauty of the world around us.

However, it is important to emphasize that being self-obsessed is not equivalent to being egotistical or self-absorbed. Instead, it is more analogous to having a strong and broad identity in which we identify closely with our self-elements. This might seem like a controversial statement or a blatant contradiction. I am seemingly comparing something negative with something we tend to consider as positive. However, self-obsession is a phenomenon that transcends duality and notions of right and wrong, good and bad. It is not *wrong* to identify with self-elements. It's not *wrong* to suffer like we do. It is just undesirable. Similarly, identity is not good or bad. It just holds within it vulnerability. A vulnerability to change.

So you and I are both self-obsessed but we needn't take it personally. There's no need to point the finger of blame inward. Neither of us chose to be self-obsessed. If you find yourself resisting the idea of being self-obsessed, ask yourself this question: "Who is it that is self-obsessed?"

It is the same Person who has psychological needs and the same Person who has a self. It is that fictional character in our minds that our brains project an identity onto. Self-obsession arises from the self-aware brain as a solution for the psychological needs that having a Person exposes. Self-obsession is not your fault – it's not actually *you* at all!

The Nature of Self-Obsession

So far, I have described our identities as consisting of high-value self-elements that we have and feel positive about. These are self-elements that we don't want to change. However, our identities and self-obsession go far beyond the things we have and like.

Imagine someone who has grown up passionately disliking an aspect of their physical appearance. It feels so significant to them that they hold strong beliefs about it, which have shaped the way they see themselves as a person. They actively identify with the very aspect of their physical appearance that they reject. This person does not fear this self-element changing, they are desperate for it to change. The fear and sadness they experience come not from change but from the prospect of things *not* changing.

Therefore, it is too simplistic to say that we suffer only because our self-elements change. It is more accurate to say that we suffer because we identify with a self-element and are then resistant to "what is", whether that be an unwelcome change or unwelcome continuity. In either case, it is a pain caused by desire – a desire for things to be different from how they are.

It's not just the self-elements that we have that cause us problems. Imagine somebody growing up in a family where academic achievement is considered critical, both in terms of status and as a measure of success. They work incredibly hard at school and spend much of their weekends reading textbooks. Despite their best efforts, their grades are average. While they excel at sports, they cannot match what they do in the classroom with what they do on the football pitch. Their parents are deeply concerned, demanding that their child work even harder, warning them that failure at school will have far-reaching consequences in later life. And yet, despite working harder, their grades do not improve. The only noticeable change is a sharp decline in their self-esteem that they go on to struggle with for decades.

If this person was reading this book they might conclude that they identify strongly with "being stupid". However, this would not be the case. In fact, they would be identifying with not being academically gifted. This distinction may seem trivial at first glance, but it is critical when it comes to how this person feels about themselves.

Identifying with things we perceive not to be or not to have is very common. Interestingly, as the next example shows, this doesn't always have to be something we want.

Imagine somebody loses a parent at a young age due to a heart attack. It is an experience that has a profound impact on them. In their grief, they read books about the heart to understand how something so terrible might have happened. They read about the hereditary nature of cardiovascular disease and worry they may also suffer the same fate as their parent. As their concerns grow, they become preoccupied with thoughts about their health and visit their doctor frequently for check-ups. They are told they have illness anxiety, but this does little to quell their fears. Over time, they develop a deep-rooted belief that they are seriously unwell and convinced their doctor must be incompetent. They spend much of their time checking for signs of serious illness and monitoring vital signs like blood pressure and heart rate.

Illness anxiety, or hypochondriasis, is a relatively common problem which demonstrates the final face of self-obsession. In this example, the person's self-obsession was initially centred around not being sick or becoming sick. The fear of becoming seriously ill became so pervasive that not being sick became a fundamental part of who they were. They became hyper-vigilant for signs they might be ill and increasingly paranoid that a catastrophic medical problem may be developing undiagnosed. Over time they began to identify with actually being ill, which illustrates how self-obsession can evolve.

Like our other examples, this person was unable to accept things as they were. At first, they struggled to come to terms with the possibility they could become sick. Later, they could not accept that they weren't. Paradoxically, their obsession with not being ill actually led to a medical disorder, albeit one of the mind rather than the catastrophic physical health issue they were convinced they had.

In total, there are four ways that self-obsession manifests. These are shown in the self-obsession grid below. Every aspect of our selves that we identify with will fit within one of these four categories.

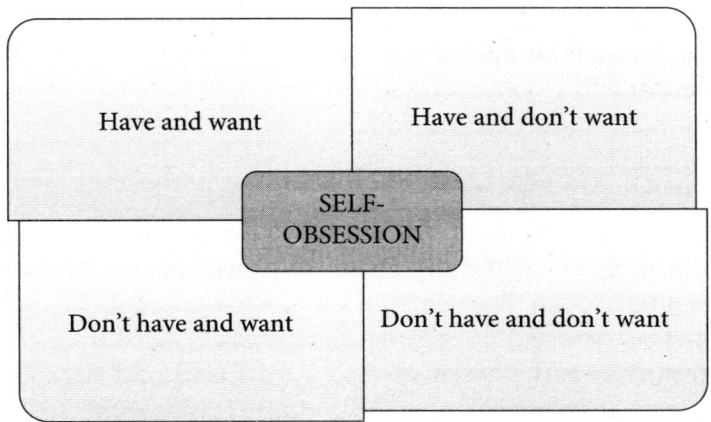

Self-Obsession and Complex Needs

In the last chapter we said that a need becomes unmet when a self-element we have changes in a way that no longer fulfils this need. We also experience an unmet need if we identify with something that we don't have but decide that we need. This could be something that we previously had and lost or something we've never had.

Something that we identify as having and not wanting tends to be interpreted by our brains in much the same way as something we don't have and want. This is usually because we tend to wish that something we did want was in its place. For example, we may identify as being overweight while wishing we were slim. Whether our focus is more directed at what we have and don't like or don't have and want depends on how we perceive the self-element in question. In either case, there's a desire for things to be other than what they are.

A self-element we identify as having and not wanting may represent a threat because of the knock-on effect on other self-elements that fulfil important needs. Similarly, things that we do not have and do not want are potential threats. This is because if something happened and we were to somehow obtain these things, we would be left with the same problem caused by the things we have and don't want! Are you still with me . . .?!

The Evolution of Self-Obsession

When I think of the evolution of conscious awareness, I imagine Charles Darwin himself gradually cranking up a self-awareness dial. I see him peering down (weirdly biblical, I know!) at early humans living simple lives and thinking, "They could probably take a little more". Perhaps after 30,000 years or so, he'd reassess the situation and crank up the dial further. "Just a little more." Maybe this would keep going for a few hundred thousand years. Finally, Darwin would look down at these sophisticated apes and think, "I've gone this far, I may as well go all the way!" He'd then turn the conscious awareness dial all the way up. About 10,000 years later, he may take a sneaky peek to see if everything is alright and look down, horrified, thinking, "Holy ****, what have I done?!"

The evolution of self-awareness has boosted human survival chances by acting as a powerful incentive to make our ancestors *want* to live rather than simply having the instinct to survive. Of course, evolution acts without an intention or master plan. As much as I might imagine Darwin "playing God", there is no one making any conscious decisions. Evolution can't predict the future so couldn't have foreseen the rapid development of human civilization, society, culture and technology. Evolution also couldn't have anticipated that the consciously aware brain would create such an innovative solution to make sense of its own awareness: a character I refer to as our Person whom we presume is the source of our conscious awareness. Evolution wasn't responsible for us believing that we are our Persons. It was us, not evolution, who converted our instinctual wants into psychological needs leading to the creation of a self for us to identify with and obsess over.

The human condition appears to be too bizarre and self-defeating to have arisen purely through evolution. A genetic susceptibility to self-obsession is almost certainly exacerbated by biological systems, which reinforce our tendency to self-obsess through biochemical "carrots" and "sticks". However, self-obsession is a phenomenon that transcends science.

Culture of Self-Obsession

For most of us self-obsession is unavoidable, especially those living in a Western, individualistic society. It is actively encouraged from the moment we gain enough self-awareness to realize we exist. We are immediately given the name of our Person and its importance is continuously reinforced thereafter. This, together with our biological instincts running in the background, makes self-obsession unescapable. Here are some of the ways we're encouraged to self-obsess.

Physical Appearance

From beauty standards magnified in the media and advertising worlds to social media and celebrity culture, there's little wonder why so many of us feel that looking good is a critical need and physical appearance represents an important aspect of identity. Countless young people today grow up believing that to be beautiful is to be happy. Many of us hold idealized images regarding what it is to be pretty or handsome. How many people look at themselves in the mirror and feel good enough? Should we be surprised that eight per cent of the global population will experience an eating disorder in their lifetimes?[3]

Status

Not only should we be attractive but we should also be successful. Many of us live in a culture where there's a strong emphasis on academic and career success as critical determinants of personal worth and social esteem. We *need* to be successful and we *need* to be recognized as such. This leads to an endless pursuit of wealth and social recognition that some feel they can earn by driving fast cars or having big houses. Living in a materialistic world means that self-worth can quickly become dependent on external validation and achievement.

The obsession with status is seemingly supported by research by Anderson et al., (2023) exploring the prevalence of work addiction, sometimes referred to as workaholism. The study concluded that around one in seven people are affected by a constant need to work[4].

Romantic Ideals

How many of us desperately search for our other half – our perfect partner? Our favourite films and books show us what relationships should be like and we believe this is what we need in order to be happy. We develop clear ideas about what a good relationship feels like and we become preoccupied with our search for the right one.

Many people believe that being single is a problem and their obsession with either being or not being in a relationship dominates their lives. We feel the need to be loved romantically and rely on our partners for self-worth and to give meaning to our lives. We constantly compare partners to the romantic ideals we hold in our heads and feel discontented when they fail to live up to our unrealistically high expectations.

Self-Help

Go into any bookstore and you'll be presented with a wall of books promoting self-growth, self-discovery, self-improvement and self-development. All are offering novel solutions to help us become better versions of ourselves. Never before has the spotlight been more focused on who we are and what we identify with. We hold an image in our heads of the person we want to become. We want that person to be *more* successful, *more* fun and *more* outgoing. These seem like worthy pursuits that our friends and families encourage. But the more we try to improve ourselves, the more we are reinforcing the belief that who we are is in some way inadequate. Our longing to change leads to us becoming stuck in self-critical thinking patterns and cycles of depression.

Individuality

It is not enough to just have an identity, we must have a *strong* identity that distinguishes us from others and shows we're unique. We're actively encouraged in today's society to identify with as many aspects of ourselves as we can because identity gives us individuality and individuality makes us significant. We are told to stand out even though many of us are desperate to simply *belong*. This leaves us in a double bind, where our instincts clash with our beliefs.

"Will I feel like I don't belong if I don't stand out?"

The pursuit of individuality is driven by an underlying fear of irrelevance. We're afraid of fading into the background and living a meaningless life. Existential angst can haunt us and we cling to our identity to give us purpose.

Closing Thoughts

For a child born in the world today, self-obsession is a rite of passage. Our individualistic and self-obsessed culture actively promotes self-obsession and society is dominated by the self-obsessed. While we may be born with a genetic vulnerability to self-obsession, the socio-cultural landscape in which we live makes it impossible to avoid.

Of course, self-obsession does not happen overnight. It is a gradual conditioning that starts in childhood. At an early age we're taught the importance of individuality. Most of us are lucky enough to be told we're special and our families help us create our early identity. At school we begin to compare ourselves with others. This starts in the classroom but extends on to social media. We quickly learn where our inadequacies lie. We become fixated on things we are not while desperately trying to cling to aspects of our selves that we do value.

We learn about what we must strive for to be happy. Influential figures like our parents and teachers urge us to work hard at school and reward us when our grades are good. We're told that academic success leads to a happy future. A good job gives us money and status. Money helps us accumulate things that will improve our lives, things we think we need that are highlighted by manipulative marketing. Status gives us a sense of belonging and respect from others.

We learn what to look for in a relationship and what qualities to expect in a partner. Being single is an option but most of us believe our lives are lacking if we do not have a romantic partner. Better still is having a family of our own. Children give our lives meaning and a greater sense of identity.

We are told that we can be anything we want. We are just as obsessed with the person we are as the person we are not. We are obsessed with what we have and what we lack. We self-obsess in the hope of finding happiness, yet self-obsession becomes our greatest obstacle. The more self-obsessed we become, the more pain we experience. This makes us focus even more intensely on our selves in the hope of finding the problem. But our focus on the self *is* the problem in the first place, so our efforts only worsen the situation. We become caught in a spiral of self-obsession and worsening psychological pain.

In the midst of this spiral, we can find ourselves sitting in the waiting rooms of doctors' surgeries, desperate for answers. It is the doctors' surgery we go to now, in the final chapter of Part 1, as we look to establish a direct link between self-obsession and the mental health disorders that so many of us struggle with during our lives.

Here's our fourth deduction:

The degree to which we suffer is proportional to the extent to which our Person identifies with self-elements (self-obsesses).

REFLECTION

On multi-day hiking trips, I like to take at least one photograph each day. It makes me more mindful of my surroundings and appreciative of beauty I may otherwise miss. I particularly love walking beside rivers and lakes because reflections of the sky and trees make for interesting compositions. If the water's surface is still enough, it's hard to know where the sky ends and the water begins.

When we look at a reflection on the surface of the water, we witness a double reflection. This is because everything we see is already a reflection of our own perception. Nothing we experience is uninfluenced by our minds. What we look at as reality is never more than *our* reality. We do not see what our eyes see. We see what our brains tell us our eyes see. While seeing is believing, what we believe depends on what our brains tell us. We cannot observe the world through unbiased eyes. Only the eyes of an animal see it for what it is, yet they're not aware of what they see, so they can never tell us what the world's truly like. All we can do is gaze out upon it as we do upon the surface of a shimmering lake and wonder in awe at what is reflected back.

"When the mind constantly runs after the wandering senses, it drives away wisdom, like the wind blowing a ship off course."

Krishna

EXTRAORDINARY MISERY

Sigmund Freud once said that the role of psychoanalysis was to "turn extraordinary misery into ordinary unhappiness". I've always found this to be a brilliant quote, not because I agree with it but because it is such an interesting perspective. To consider our everyday existence as being "ordinarily unhappy" is an incredibly bleak take on humanity yet I can understand what he's getting at! To live our lives in the self-obsessed manner that most of us do is indeed inherently painful, being dominated by stress and punctuated by loss.

To call this suffering ordinary is to suggest it is normal. Is being normally unhappy the best we can hope for? If we accept self-obsession as our best outcome, this might be true. However, I believe we should be setting our sights on something much greater: *extraordinary happiness.*

We will look at how we can get there, but first we must take our discussion of self-obsession to its logical conclusion. We must understand why for some of us, self-obsession gives rise to overwhelming levels of anxiety and despair. It's time to understand self-obsession's role in the extraordinary misery that Freud often encountered in his clinics.

Self-Obsession Self-Perpetuates

When I worked in general practice, I frequently saw people who were struggling with their mental health. When I asked them how they were feeling, I was often struck by how similar their experiences were. Many described a sense of helplessness, a feeling they were being controlled by something stronger than they were: "I feel overcome by worry. It's like being engulfed by a cloud of despair."

When I compared their accounts to my experience of panic attacks and depression, I could relate to the powerlessness they were describing. There's the sense that things snowball, with anxiety and mood becoming progressively worse over time.

The feeling that our struggles intensify gives us a clue as to the nature of the mechanism underlying the problem, a cycle that is self-perpetuating. The cycle begins and ends with self-obsession, giving rise to the extraordinary misery many of us experience that often manifests as anxiety disorders and depression.

The Self-Obsession Cycle

As we've seen, the cycle begins with us identifying strongly with the self. Critically, we identify with self-elements that we either "don't have and want" or "have and don't want". For example, this could be the partner we no longer have or the status that we long for. In either case, there's a desire for our self to be something other than what it is.

Critical to this self-obsession is our deeply held belief about what our psychological needs look like and which self-elements are necessary to satisfy them. As our brains assess the self-elements in question, they evaluate whether they are fulfilling their essential functions. These self-elements are things we either don't like about our selves or things we wished we had, so our brains conclude there's a problem in the self because of the disparity between what it should be and what it is.

This deficiency is felt in our conscious awareness as negativity toward ourselves and specific aspects of our lives. With deficiencies exposed and our needs unfulfilled, our brains look to correct the problem. This increases our focus on the self-elements under scrutiny, making us more self-obsessed. This in turn reinforces our beliefs that these self-elements must be really important since they are all we think about and are associated with so much heartache.

The result is increasing self-obsession, falling self-perception (how we feel about ourselves) and deteriorating mental wellbeing. As the cycle continues, distress mounts until the issues many recognize as anxiety disorders and depression emerge.

This is what the self-obsession cycle looks like:

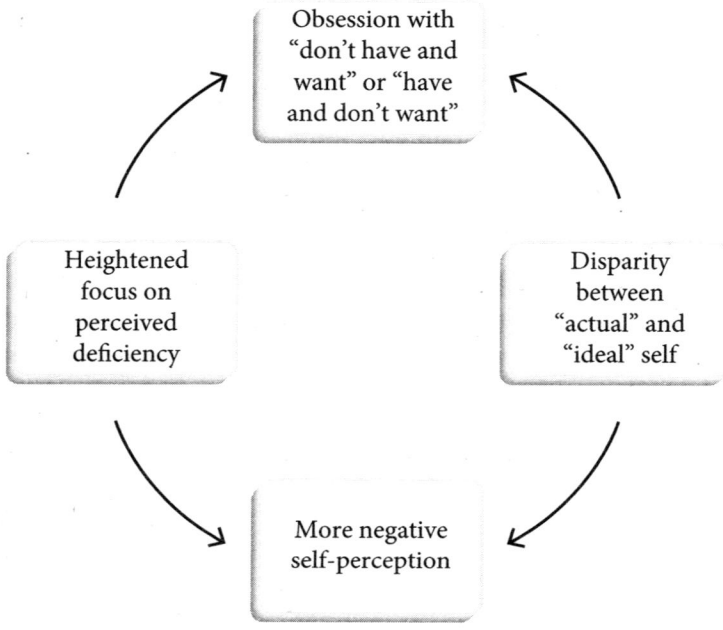

Why is it that anxiety and depression feel and look so different despite being produced by the same cycle? To understand why, we must examine the cycle more closely to see how different problems can emerge from the same underlying process.

Start of the Cycle

In depression, the self-obsession cycle may arise gradually or as a result of a sudden change event. Typically, this change event involves the loss (actual or perceived) of something we felt was ours and that we valued highly. This could be anything, but classically, changes to our relationships (romantic or otherwise), jobs and physical health act as important triggers.

Alternatively, for those who experience more insidious symptoms of depression, the cycle tends to begin either in response to gradually changing self-elements or slowly evolving beliefs. For example, somebody in an emotionally abusive relationship might begin to believe criticisms their partner voices about their character. Their *personality* self-element would become more negatively evaluated over time.

Whether the cycle powers up slowly or quickly matters little insofar as the result is the same: reduced self-perception. This pattern of onset seen in depression is also commonly observed in people struggling with anxiety. While some report gradually worsening feelings of anxiety over many months and even years, others report a more sudden onset of symptoms associated with a change event. This may be one that has a sudden negative impact on their self-belief. For example, imagine somebody failing what they perceive to be an important exam. This failure could immediately change how they perceive their *education* self-element. If this served to meet a critical psychological need for this individual, then this change could quickly impact their self-perception by exposing a disparity between what the self-element is and what it should be.

Triggers and Causes

When it comes to describing the onset of the self-obsession cycle in anxiety and depression, the use of language is important. When people describe their struggles, they naturally look to identify the cause and often wrongly attribute blame. We assume depression is caused by the breakdown of a relationship or the loss of a job. We assume anxiety is caused by an upcoming exam or the prospect of humiliating ourselves while giving a presentation at work. This seems like logical cause and effect when in fact these events are simply triggers which expose a person's underlying self-obsession. The self-obsession that was lying dormant is the true cause of their psychological distress. The trigger was simply the straw that broke the camel's back.

The Two Sides of Self-Perception

Once the self-obsession cycle has been ignited, our self-perception inevitably takes a hit. The brain sees a disparity between what is and what should be and concludes that there's a deficiency within the self. At the point of self-perception, self-obsession "decides" to take an anxious or depressive path.

This decision is determined by how the brain interprets the deficiency it sees. This is likely decided by the deeply held beliefs a person holds about themselves, heavily influenced by certain character traits. These factors give each of us an intrinsic vulnerability to either seeing ourselves as not good enough or not able enough. This means that when we suffer a knock to our self-perception, some people will be more likely to experience feelings of low self-worth, and others will be more prone to feelings of low self-assurance. Here, low self-assurance incorporates things like low self-confidence and low self-belief.

In effect, the self-obsession cycle swings like a pendulum toward either anxiety or depression, depending on our inherent bias toward the two states. As the cycle self-perpetuates, this bias is then interpreted by the brain as either representing an ongoing threat or unmet need. This accounts for the difference in symptoms between anxiety and depression.

While each of us have a natural vulnerability to either anxiety or depression, we do not necessarily experience one or the other. Low self-perception will be impacted by the nature of whatever triggers it. For example, a significant loss event can push the self-perception pendulum toward depression regardless of its natural leaning due to the force of its impact. Furthermore, as the self-obsession cycle gathers pace, it affects self-perception in all aspects. What may begin as low self-assurance will inevitably begin to impact self-worth if self-perception continues to fall. Similarly, plummeting self-worth will invariably undermine self-assurance sooner or later. This explains why the risk of developing anxiety is higher if you have depression and vice versa. Anxiety and depression are not mutually exclusive states, even if we have a natural propensity toward one or the other.

Catalysts of the Self-Obsession Cycle

Falling self-perception is not the only factor driving the self-obsession cycle. The cycle is also affected by how we think and behave and changes in brain biochemistry. These act by increasing self-obsession through their impact on our self-perception and emotional state.

The complete cycle looks like this:

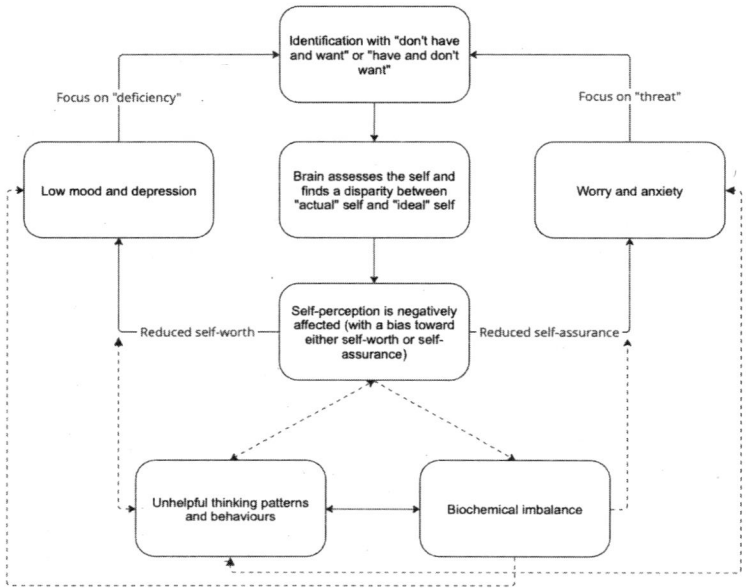

The dashed lines in the model highlight the catalytic effects of these additional factors on the self-obsession cycle. As self-perception falls, a person's thinking tends to become progressively more self-critical and their behaviours increasingly self-destructive. This leads to worsening self-perception and deepening emotional distress. How someone thinks and behaves also affects their brain biochemistry. Changes here will increase their susceptibility to unhelpful thinking patterns and behaviours while also directly contributing to deteriorating mood and heightened feelings of anxiety. Whenever there is sustained emotional distress, maladaptive thinking patterns and behaviours invariably develop and become increasingly entrenched.

Ultimately, every component within the self-obsession cycle acts as both a cause and an effect, reinforcing the others in a continuous loop. Each factor drives the cycle forward and amplifies the impact of others, creating a powerful self-perpetuating system. The result is one of deepening psychological distress fuelled by increasing self-obsession. To better understand this system, let's look at the components described here in more detail.

Unhelpful Thinking Patterns

Negative thinking in depression is well known. The psychiatrist Aaron Beck (1979) described depression as involving a negative cognitive triad, incorporating negative thoughts about oneself, the future and the world around us[5].

Negative thoughts about ourselves that are seen in depression often arise from feelings of guilt and shame. These feelings give rise to thoughts like "I am a total failure" or "everything about me is bad". In cognitive behavioural therapy (CBT), these negative thinking patterns are known as cognitive distortions or thinking errors. Here, the deduction that *everything* about them is bad or they are a *total* failure is an example of over generalization, where a person takes one event or characteristic and unreasonably applies it to all aspects of their life.

Negative thinking about the future is linked to feelings of hopelessness and helplessness. Thoughts like, "It's certain to go wrong", are particularly common. This is a way of thinking known as fortune telling, where a person predicts that events will turn out badly without any evidence or basis for this conclusion. The same feeling of hopelessness can also lead to thoughts like, "there's nothing good in the world". This is an example of mental filtering, where a person focuses exclusively on the negative sides of a situation while ignoring any positive or neutral aspects.

In depression, the negativity of thinking is heavily influenced by how unhappy we are feeling. The worse we feel, the more pervasive our negative thinking tends to become and the surer we are that our negative thoughts are accurate. This phenomenon is sometimes called emotional reasoning, where strong feelings are taken as evidence to validate our negative thinking. After all, it stands to reason that if we feel *this* ashamed, something *must* be fundamentally wrong with us.

Many of the same unhelpful thinking patterns we have discussed in relation to depression are also seen in anxiety. For example, fortune telling is common, as the anxious mind is all too willing to predict unfortunate outcomes regardless of their likelihood. An extreme version of this is catastrophization, which describes the tendency to predict the worst-case scenario. It is often associated with so-called "what if" thoughts that may escalate to a person imagining disastrous outcomes arising from even a benign situation.

When mistakes or unfortunate situations do occur, there is often an assumption that whatever has gone wrong is our fault, which is known as personalization. Frequently attributing negative outcomes or events as being our doing will erode our self-perception even further.

The more negatively we think, the worse we'll feel. Negative thinking keeps our attention on the self-element that has the perceived deficiency. Therefore, negative thinking is a product of the self-obsession cycle and a key driver of it.

Unhelpful Behaviours

A similar picture can be seen in our behaviours. As our mood deteriorates in depression, we tend to withdraw from the world and become increasingly isolated. When we feel down, apathetic and negative about ourselves, the last thing we feel like is going out and about – especially if other people are involved. After all, if we are so fed up with our own company, why would anyone else want to spend time with us?

However, shutting ourselves away makes us feel even worse. We have no positive interactions with people and don't give ourselves a chance to enjoy ourselves. Without positive reinforcement, we feel even more miserable, telling ourselves we were right not to inflict this sorrow on anybody else. To make matters worse, the more we hide away, the more people assume we don't want to see them. Eventually, this may mean we lose friends, further reinforcing the belief that we are worthless.

Doing less often involves exercising less. This is exacerbated by our low energy levels, reduced motivation and negative self-perception. Staying active can seem pointless and far more bother than it is worth. However, this further compounds the situation because we don't receive the benefits from endorphins that help offset some feelings of low mood. We also miss out on cognitive benefits such as improved concentration, which would boost our self-assurance.

Locked in the vicious cycle of self-obsession, we can struggle to cope with the constant self-hate and despair that we feel. This can make us look for short-term relief to either distract us from our pain or dampen it. For many this involves turning to alcohol. However, alcohol is a depressant, which means rather than helping us feel better, it perpetuates the self-obsession cycle. This is made worse by the other effects of alcohol, like disrupted sleep, impaired judgement and negative impacts on our self-worth.

Like depression, many of the same unhelpful behaviours can perpetuate the self-obsession cycle seen in anxiety. Where we saw social withdrawal and isolation in depression, in anxiety it is referred to as avoidance. When we are feeling anxious, our instinct is often to avoid any situations that may trigger our anxiety. This response is normal and represents a relic from our fight or flight system designed to protect us from danger. However, for most of us the situations we fear are not life-threatening. Instead, they are situations where we feel under personal attack.

For example, people with social anxiety disorder tend to avoid social situations because they think this will protect them from potential humiliation or being exposed as socially inadequate. This tends to be fuelled by low self-assurance, making them feel vulnerable in these settings and doubtful of their ability to cope. However, while avoidance will provide temporary relief from their anxiety, it will not help them challenge the belief that they will embarrass themselves or that they are socially inept. Instead, it reinforces the belief that the only way they can cope is to do their best to avoid social situations altogether. Over time, avoidance leads to a progressively more negative self-perception and worsening anxiety, perhaps even when among close friends.

As the self-obsession cycle gathers pace, it is easy for someone to feel increasingly overwhelmed. Their life might feel like it is shrinking around them as they begin avoiding more things. Naturally, they look for solutions. Short-term coping mechanisms, like alcohol, may seem like a good option. But while alcohol may provide some Dutch courage in certain situations, it invariably leads to heightened anxiety levels. This is because its sedating effects are lost as it's metabolized and the body experiences a rebound effect where symptoms of anxiety return stronger than before. Having a reliance on alcohol reinforces the belief that without it, things would be unmanageable. This further undermines self-perception and leads to feelings of helplessness and low self-worth.

Inactivity can also be associated with anxiety disorders, especially those where a person's physical symptoms play important roles. For example, someone with panic disorder may become concerned about the health of their heart. This may make them avoid exertion altogether out of fear of developing symptoms of panic or the effect that increasing their heart rate may have on their bodies. This lack of exercise not only means they miss out on the natural stress-relieving benefits of endorphins but it also fails to provide any counter-evidence to challenge their misguided belief that exercise is harmful to their health.

The behaviours seen in anxiety are commonly referred to as safety behaviours. They are things we do that we think will keep us safe from harm. However, there is no actual harm to avoid and our actions serve only to worsen our anxiety. While avoidance may give us temporary feelings of security, we're making ourselves more vulnerable because our self-assurance is undermined.

The Role of Biochemistry

This last catalyst in the self-obsession cycle is one which most divides opinion. The role of biochemistry in the development and exacerbation of anxiety disorders and depression is a hotly debated topic, as is the use of anti-depressants.

Firstly, it is clear that brain chemistry influences how we feel. In a sense, everything we experience is chemistry. Every thought, feeling and emotion involves chemicals moving across synapses in our brain. We know that certain chemicals such as serotonin, dopamine and noradrenaline play essential roles in regulating how we feel.

Studies have shown that serotonin levels, for example, are often low in people experiencing anxiety and low mood. This has allowed us to develop a specific class of anti-depressants called Selective Serotonin Reuptake Inhibitors (SSRIs), which increase the concentration of serotonin in critical parts of the brain. These drugs can and do improve symptoms of anxiety and depression.

However, they don't work for everyone. Not everybody who is depressed has low serotonin. Even those who do don't always find that their depression improves when serotonin levels increase. The same is true for anxiety and a similar pattern is seen in how patients respond to other anti-depressant and anxiolytic medications. Sometimes they work, sometimes they don't. Sometimes, one type of anti-depressant helps someone, while another makes little or no difference.

The relationship between the dysregulation of chemicals in the brain and anxiety and depression is therefore inconclusive. We cannot say that these disorders are caused by biochemical disruption. However, biochemical disruption does play an important role for some people.

My hypothesis is that chemical imbalance plays more of a catalytic role in the self-obsession cycles of some than others. This is likely most dependent on the speed at which the cycle is spinning. A faster spinning cycle is associated with greater levels of distress. Since anti-depressants are only ever effective in moderate to severe anxiety and depression, this suggests that the speed of the cycle affects how much influence biochemistry has. The way that each of us responds to anti-depressants is also affected by our genetics since we respond differently to drugs thanks to genetic variation.

For those they do help, the benefit of anti-depressants should not be underestimated. For some, they provide the relief a person needs to begin to turn things around.

The Cycle Grows

Left unchecked, the self-obsession cycle tends to accelerate. I sometimes imagine it like a tornado that gradually builds in strength and spins faster and faster. Like a tornado engulfs things in its path, the self-obsession cycle consumes other aspects of the self. Soon, even self-elements we have and value become caught up in the cycle's not-so-loving embrace.

This is why anxiety is so often associated with fear of failure and loss. The low self-assurance that results from the self-obsession cycle makes us overestimate threats to other self-elements and underestimate our ability to cope with them. The self-obsession cycle changes our beliefs about the importance of specific self-elements and our relationship with them. In depression, the belief that we are worthless can spread as a wave of negativity right across the self. Even elements we were once proud of can look increasingly deficient.

People often describe the feeling of being consumed by their negativity or anxiety. This feeling is caused by the self-obsession cycle wreaking havoc in every corner of the self. What starts as a localized skirmish becomes a full-scale war that you find yourself stuck right in the middle of.

Self-Obsession is Misdiagnosed

Feeling increasingly overwhelmed, many of us find ourselves sitting in front of our doctor, desperately hoping for some kind of relief.

Doctor: "How can I help?"
Patient: "I think I might be depressed."
Doctor: "What makes you think that?"
Patient: "I feel depressed."
Doctor: "Has anything happened?"
Patient: "Nothing special."
Doctor: "Are you still enjoying your hobbies?"
Patient: "I don't enjoy anything anymore."
Doctor: "How do you feel about yourself?"
Patient: "Rubbish."
Doctor: "How's your sleep and appetite?"
Patient: "I barely sleep despite feeling drained and have lost my appetite."
Doctor: "Sounds like you're depressed."
Patient: "That's what I told you!"

Here, the patient tells their doctor they feel depressed and is then told that they *are* depressed. Depression is seemingly the cause of their problem and the problem itself! This doesn't make sense. It would be like telling your doctor that you have a cough and then being told that your cough was caused by the cough itself. Most of us would feel perplexed by this explanation and ask whether there might be something else going on that may be causing this cough, like a chest infection.

This is because a cough is a symptom. In the same way anxiety and depression are symptoms. Anxiety isn't caused by an anxiety disorder and depression isn't caused by depression. They are both caused by self-obsession. They are the same problem expressed in different ways. This is why the same medications are recommended for both – they're treating the same condition, the *human condition*.

If someone were to ask their doctor why they were experiencing anxiety or depression, they would be told a variation of what I was taught in my medical training: "They're caused by a combination of biological, psychological and social factors."

This is the so-called biopsychosocial model that explains the pathophysiology of psychological illness. It says anxiety and depression are caused by a combination of your body, your mind and the world around you – everything basically. The medical community could save a lot of time by holding their hands up and simply saying, "We don't know why this is happening". This is probably more sensible than telling patients that they're self-obsessed though. It may take more than a ten-minute consultation to explain their way out of that!

Closing Thoughts

And so there we have it. Self-obsession is the cause of the psychological pain we experience as part of the human condition. It is through the self-obsession cycle that ordinary unhappiness is elevated into the extra-ordinary misery that so many of us experience as anxiety and depression.

From conscious awareness to self-awareness to self-obsession, we have each been on quite a journey. We're now ready for our fifth and final deduction:

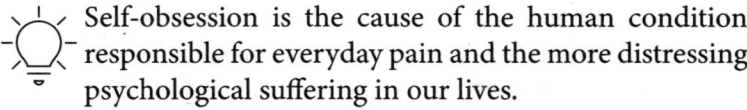 Self-obsession is the cause of the human condition responsible for everyday pain and the more distressing psychological suffering in our lives.

You and I have both lived our lives bound by the chains of self-obsession. These chains have felt so familiar that many people believe that they can never be broken. But they are wrong. Freud was wrong. The human condition is not a life sentence. There is freedom waiting for us all, a freedom each of us deserves. All we need to do is open our eyes to reality and let go of the Person that our brains try so desperately to cling to.

REFLECTION

Taoists believe life should be approached with a sense of flow and harmony, aligning with the natural course of things rather than resisting or forcing change. The Taoist path is often called the "Watercourse Way" since water always seeks a natural path, not forcing against obstacles but rather flowing around them.

Water is content just to be water.

What are you content to *just* be?

What are you content *not* to be?

*"Men are disturbed,
not by things,
but by the principles
and notions
which they form
concerning things."*

Epictetus

PART II

SETTING YOUR SIGHTS ON FREEDOM

The path to overcoming self-obsession has two distinct stages, reflecting two contrasting philosophical models for understanding the human mind. Stage one of the journey reduces self-obsession to overcome psychological distress. Stage two leads us beyond self-obsession to a state of mental wellness most of us would never have imagined possible. While I describe these as sequential stages, it is important to remember that all the methods discussed in subsequent chapters can and should be practised simultaneously. If we can overcome self-obsession a little, we'll experience some freedom. If we can overcome self-obsession completely, we'll experience total freedom. It is up to you how far you're willing to go.

Stage One

Stage one is most consistent with the aims of Western psychology. Here, we are working on the assumption that we *are* our Person. In other words, I am Tom and I have a self that I feel positively or negatively toward. In this model, how I feel about Tom (or "myself" without the gap) is a direct reflection of how I feel about my objective self, a self that encompasses my individual self-elements. The goals of stage one are to slow down the self-obsession cycle by overcoming negative self-perception while also reducing the extent to which we identify with self-elements. These two goals are linked because slowing the self-obsession cycle will naturally reduce our focus on the self and letting go of self-elements will help stop the self-obsession cycle from being activated.

In stage one, we are effectively looking to take ourselves from Freud's "extraordinary misery" to the "ordinary unhappiness" he believed was the best we can hope for as humans. This stage should not be underestimated. For those of us who are significantly self-obsessed (and that's most of us!), this will make a huge difference to how we are feeling, especially if we're struggling with anxiety or depression.

However, this stage can only take us so far because we are limited by the assumption that we *are* our Person. By being our Person, we will continue to have psychological needs we feel must be met in order for us to be "happy". This means that, while we can significantly reduce our grip on self-elements, we will not be able to let go of them completely since we will still be relying on them to fulfil our needs. Threats to our self will not be felt as acutely and loss events won't hurt as much but we will nevertheless still be vulnerable to change. We will be less self-obsessed but only partially free.

Stage Two

For us to be totally free, we must go somewhere that psychology cannot take us. In stage one, we are still clinging to the misguided assumption that we *are* our Person – that it is Tom who is consciously aware and that I experience my life as Tom.

Fortunately for us, and unfortunately for psychology, Freud was wrong, and the way most psychologists see the human experience continues to be wrong today. The fact is, it is not our Person who is consciously aware, but rather, it is us who is aware of our Person. Tom actually arises from conscious awareness itself rather than the other way around. While this distinction may at first glance appear subtle, it is critical for us to understand it if we want to free ourselves from self-obsession.

Earlier in the book, when I discussed *who* is consciously aware, I mischievously said "nobody" to emphasize that it isn't our Person. However, this is not totally true. It is not nobody who is aware of your Person – it is actually *you* – the *real* you! This is the you that has been obscured since early childhood by the Person you believe you are. It is the you that you were born as and the you that has been here all along. This you has many names, but I like to call it our "true nature" – or the real Tom that is beneath the version of Tom I've been pretending to be most of my life!

Interestingly, this true nature is not exclusively human. Every animal is born with its own unique and instinctive way of responding to its environment. This can be observed in a litter of puppies. No two puppies are the same, where one may be timid, another may be boisterous. This gives us the impression that our pets have their own personalities. This is a direct observation of their nature that our pets are not consciously aware of. The same can be seen in babies, born with intrinsic individuality, that we observe in the different ways they react to things. As infants become consciously aware, this nature then begins to influence the way the child makes sense of the world. It also helps to shape the Person they begin to become. However, as the self-obsession machinery grinds into gear, children start to develop beliefs about what their psychological needs are and what their Persons (which they perceive as themselves) should and shouldn't be. Unfortunately, with the child experiencing the world through self-obsessed eyes, there's an inevitable drift away from their true nature.

Stage two of our journey is about returning home – connecting with our true nature and letting go of the Person we have been wedded to for much of our lives. As we free ourselves, we will escape our psychological needs and overcome reliance on our self-elements. This will allow us to let go of the self completely, breaking the self-obsession cycle and freeing us from the human condition.

What Does it Look Like to Be Free?

The benefits of overcoming self-obsession are difficult to overstate in terms of our wellbeing and the effect it has on those around us. While the negative aspects of self-obsession might well provide you with the motivation you need to make changes, it is helpful to explore what being free looks like.

Becoming Healthy in Mind and Body

To escape self-obsession is to escape the self-obsession cycle and prevent anxiety disorders and depression from developing. This is because the self-obsession cycle is the cause of these problems, and where there is no cause, there can be no effect. Just like a weed cannot grow without roots, anxiety and depression cannot arise without the self-obsession cycle to provide them with a foundation.

Self-obsession is not only responsible for these so-called disorders; it also causes the everyday pain we experience. Why do we fear our relationships ending, the loss of our jobs or the fading of youth? Why do we worry we're not attractive enough, wealthy enough or respected enough? We worry because we cling to every aspect of our self in the misguided belief that these self-elements are necessary in order for us to meet our apparently essential psychological needs. Sooner or later, every self-element will change and leave us disappointed. A part of us *knows* that this is true and we feel the heaviness of this truth in every waking moment. When we overcome self-obsession, we stop trying to hold on to things that are destined to change. We realize that the self can never satisfy us, so we stop expecting it to. This frees us from everyday stress while helping to insulate us from loss.

The wellness that comes from overcoming self-obsession is far beyond any mental wellbeing that we have spent our lives striving for. It is an "extraordinary happiness" that is outside the human condition itself. The impact of living in this state on physical health is momentous. Stress is a key contributor to numerous health issues affecting every system in our bodies, from immunity and cardiovascular to reproductive health and skin. This physical health benefit will be compounded by being liberated from unhealthy coping mechanisms, such as addiction, self-harm and comfort eating, that we rely on to deal with pain caused by self-obsession.

Appreciating the Now

It is said that sadness feeds on the past and worry feeds on the future. How much time do we spend dwelling on things that have happened or agonizing about things yet to come? This is wasted time since the past cannot be changed and the future only exists in our imagination. Life happens in the now, in this present moment. In self-obsession, we're constantly looking ahead for potential threats, worrying about what may happen and how it could impact us. When we're not fretting about the future, we find ourselves ruminating on memories of the past. We miss out on life despite being desperate to enjoy it.

By letting go of the self, we let go of the fear of uncertainty. We accept change and stop worrying about what's to come. Things will come and go, and we'll learn to greet every new arrival with equanimity. We will appreciate what we have for the very reason it won't last. This is how many of us feel when we receive flowers. Roses are beautiful not because they live forever but because they won't! We appreciate them more, knowing they will soon die. Every aspect of the self is like those roses – gradually wilting. But rather than enjoying the fleeting beauty of what we have, we spend our time desperately trying to prevent change. No matter what we do, everything we cherish will be lost anyway! And when we are faced with this inevitable loss, we then regret not fully appreciating what we had.

This is the wonder of overcoming self-obsession. We let go of the self and we can enjoy life even more. We can appreciate every day we share with loved ones, every minute we're on holiday and every second we're alive. Living in the moment is everything since it is all we have.

When we are present in the now, our Person also dissolves. This is because our Person is a narrative that only makes sense in the context of its past and future. Without past or future, Tom is a blank page. Whenever we are truly present, we are free from our Person and every need our Person has. In the present we can lose ourselves in moments of awe and wonder to glimpse the ultimate reality beyond our Person. This reality is something each of us already experiences anytime we find ourselves fully absorbed in the now. We often only realize it has happened after the event, once self-obsession has lured us back into the familiar embrace of our Person. Self-obsession never allows us to stay present for long because of its addiction to what has happened and what is to come. As we learn to let go of our Person, more of our time will be spent enjoying the freedom of the present moment.

Finding Joy in Simplicity

Everything we have is impermanent and nothing we have is necessary. This knowledge liberates us from the materialist treadmill so many of us find ourselves on. Ask yourself: what is the value of your house, car and belongings? What purpose do they serve? *Whose* purpose do they serve?

When we escape self-obsession, there's no need for anything beyond the physiological. We don't need to strive for status, wealth or material possessions. We can bask in the simplicity of *being*. There's nowhere we have to go and nothing we have to achieve. The purpose we have found ourselves struggling toward for so long becomes unimportant – after all, it belongs to our Person and not us! Instead, we achieve meaning by existing. This is the wonderful pursuit of aimlessness, where we realize our destination is nowhere else than where we are currently standing. The void within us that makes us feel like we are "not good enough" is replaced by a serene sense of emptiness akin to the freedom we might experience when we gaze up at the stars, pondering the vastness of the universe.

Unlocking Our Inner Creativity

There's a well-known myth that claims we only use about ten per cent of our brains. In reality, our brains are constantly active, it's just that the vast majority of neurological processes happen outside of our conscious awareness. This is great because it means we can let our unconscious brains take care of things like keeping our bodies alive while our minds focus on other things.

Unfortunately, our minds spend most of their time being self-obsessed. When we're working, we're worrying about work. When we're walking, we're worrying about what time we're going to get home and whether there's something more important we should be doing. The human mind holds within it so much genius, yet most of the time it's preoccupied by meaningless noise.

Overcoming self-obsession allows us to use the human mind to its full potential, applying our intelligence more effectively and unleashing the creativity that each of us possesses. The human race is being significantly held back by self-obsession. It is the mind that is free from the Person that can truly innovate. Imagine the wonders of the world we have missed out on because the next Michelangelo was too self-obsessed to realize their potential! When I spend time with my nieces and nephews I wonder what hidden talents may be waiting to be discovered. Perhaps one of them is destined to become a gifted musician or a skilled sportsman. If they grow up remaining true to their nature, I am sure their inner potential will be realized. The only thing that could stop them would be their own beliefs about what they should be – beliefs imposed upon them by the society and culture in which they live.

Freedom From Ambition

When I was at school, my teachers told me that academic success was a critical determinant of having a good life. If I wanted to be happy, I should study hard and achieve good grades. This was the only way I would fulfil my potential. In effect, I learnt that I *needed* to achieve and I *needed* the things that this achievement would give me. For my young and impressionable brain, my teachers' arguments were compelling.

As children, we're told what our psychological needs are and taught how important it is to meet them. Not only is it important to meet them but they must be met in the *right* way. Our good grades must take us to good universities. Here, we must achieve a good degree that will enable us to get a good job. None of us are born with any idea regarding what "good" means. We learn what good is under the well-meaning direction of our parents and teachers.

Unfortunately, our role models are self-obsessed! In fact, the entire education system is self-obsessed. Schools promote academic achievement and success by teaching children that these things will increase the likelihood of future happiness and fulfilment. The flip-side of this motivational strategy is that it also teaches them that academic failure risks unhappiness and a life without meaning. This is a dangerous game to play with impressionable young minds eager to identify with various aspects of their selves. Essentially, we are each taught to be self-obsessed as if it were something we should aspire to.

We're so ignorant of this reality that even when children have to miss school due to stress caused by exam pressure, we fail to see the harm we're doing. Are the growing rates of anxiety and depression that are seen in young people really that surprising, given the environment in which the majority are being taught?

Beyond self-obsession, there's no need to strive for anything beyond what we already have. We no longer chase status or success since we know we're good enough by the simple virtue of being who we really are. Rather than being motivated by achievement, we're driven by the desire to live in a way that's true to who we actually are. This means we thrive by virtue of being authentically us, regardless of our grades in English and Maths.

Finding Meaning in Compassion

We live in a self-obsessed world driven by individuals fighting to satisfy selfish needs. This creates a huge amount of conflict since my Person's needs are invariably different to yours. If I believe my Person's needs are more important than others, I find myself competing to have them met. This competition is an important driver of the capitalist society most of us live in.

Whenever there is a "mine" and a "yours" or an "ours" and a "theirs", we find ourselves in trouble. This way of thinking puts us in direct conflict with others. It creates intolerance because to be an individual is to be "other" than somebody else. Whenever we see people as "other" or *foreign,* we risk treating them as inferior in some way to us. This is the price of individuality that we so often herald as "good". Individuality is a direct product of self-obsession and our attachment to our Person. The individualistic mindset leads to an intolerant mindset. It is this that is responsible for the discriminatory beliefs and behaviours that permeate society.

Self-obsession not only makes us unhappy but spreads pain to others. Beyond self-obsession, there's compassion for everyone, including ourselves and people we may not know. We realize we are fundamentally the same and the illusion of separation is lost. This will make us more empathetic and accepting of others.

The Path to Freedom

You've been trapped in a self-obsessed cage for so long that it's all you have ever known. But this cage is not your true home and the door is open. If you step outside, you'll find yourself in the garden of your own house – the place where you truly belong.

Break the self-obsession cycle to free yourself from psychological pain. Overcome self-obsession to set yourself free. This is the ultimate path that is ready to welcome you once you change the way you see yourself and the world around you. This can be achieved by the following treatment approach, which encompasses the two stages we described earlier:

1. Improve your self-perception.
2. Let go of your self.
3. Find freedom from your Person.
4. Return to your true nature.

Each of these four aspects of treatment should be practised simultaneously since they facilitate one another. Together, they will take you home.

Closing Thoughts

As I write this chapter, I'm reminded of a period in my life when I was overwhelmed by anxiety and stress. I was working in an emergency department at a west London hospital. I was in the midst of burnout and reaching a point where I could no longer function. During these difficult months, I was living in staff accommodation next to the hospital, directly opposite the entrance to the ambulance bay. Every night when I lay awake in bed tormented by worry, I'd watch the blue lights of sirens dance across my bedroom walls. In my mind I'd go over the patients I'd seen that day, paranoid I'd made a mistake. I worried about what I did and didn't do, and about what would happen or not happen the next day. I was worried about everything. It felt like I was living in a nightmare and I was desperately unhappy.

The room I was living in had a single bed, desk and sink. It reminded me of a prison cell but ironically, this room was the only place I felt free. As soon as I left my room, I became a prisoner, bound to a job that was destroying me. Despite how miserable I felt, I couldn't walk away. I was so strongly attached to my career as a doctor that no amount of pain could convince me to stop.

Nietzsche described how having a strong purpose in life allows a person to withstand nearly any kind of suffering or hardship. I believe this is true. However, sometimes the why doesn't justify the how. My why was linked to the deep-rooted psychological needs of my Person. I clung to my medical career to fulfil my self-obsessed needs. So strong is the power of self-obsession that I pushed myself to the point where I could no longer walk through the hospital doors. I then watched as my medical career fell apart and the aspect of my self that I identified with most strongly vanished like dew on a blade of grass. Left in its place was an emptiness of depths I had never experienced before. It was then

I realized that anxiety and depression were two facets of the same problem – two products of the self-obsession cycle that I had been stuck in for more than a decade.

REFLECTION

There is a Taoist story about a stonecutter who became dissatisfied with life and dreamed of becoming something more powerful.

Looking up at the sky, the stonecutter sees the sun and thinks how impressive it is that it can turn night into day. At that moment, he decides to become the sun.

While shining down over his kingdom, a cloud passes and blocks out his light. Impressed by the cloud's ability to overcome the sun, he decides to become a cloud.

As he drifts across the sky, casting shadows over the earth below, a great mountain rises up and breaks him apart, sending his remnants scattering across the sky.

Astonished by the mountain's capacity to disrupt even the mightiest of clouds, he decides to become a mountain.

As he stands tall, reigning over the landscape and impervious to the elements, a humble stonecutter arrives and begins chipping away at his base.

*"Why do you stay
in prison when the door
is so wide open?"*

Rumi

CRADLING YOUR PERSON

If I see myself as my Person, I will feel bad about myself as long as I perceive a disparity between how my self-elements are and how I believe they should be. The size of the gap between what I actually see and what I want to see will determine how negatively I feel about my self and, by extension, how critically I evaluate my Person. This negative evaluation will typically be expressed as either the belief that "I am not good enough" or "I am not able enough", reflecting the two faces of negative self-perception – low self-worth and low self-assurance.

When we feel we are not good enough, we are vulnerable to depression because we internalize a sense of inadequacy and failure. When we feel like we are not able enough, we are susceptible to anxiety since we begin to overestimate threats and underestimate our ability to cope with them. As our self-perception falls, we find ourselves focusing on the self-elements we perceive as insufficient, further undermining our self-perception and perpetuating the self-obsession cycle.

To slow down the self-obsession cycle, we must find a way to feel less negatively about ourselves. This is what psychology and psychotherapy strive to achieve using a variety of different therapeutic approaches. In this chapter, we are going to focus on two specific types of therapy: Cognitive Behavioural Therapy (CBT), which I have explored a little in Chapter Five, and Person-Centred Psychotherapy. Both of these therapeutic approaches can help improve our self-perception, with or without the help of a therapist. Both help us to gradually change unhelpful beliefs we have about our selves and our Person. Let's begin by exploring the CBT approach.

The Power of CBT

In CBT, as with many therapeutic models, our life experiences, especially those in childhood, are seen as critical to the way we see things. Those of us who suffer from low self-perception will usually have one or more negative, deep-rooted beliefs about ourselves that we have held since childhood. These "core beliefs", as they are called in CBT, are usually learnt in response to specific interactions or life events.

For example, a child who frequently receives criticism rather than encouragement may develop a core belief that they're inadequate or incompetent. Another who experiences neglect or a lack of affection from caregivers may believe themselves to be unlovable. These core beliefs are then held rigidly as the child moves into adulthood, irrespective of circumstances and evidence that may suggest otherwise. In the context of self-obsession these core beliefs about our Person are associated with thoughts like, "*I* am unlovable" or "*I* am incompetent".

In order to cope with having such beliefs about ourselves, we learn to live according to certain rules. These rules are designed to keep us safe by helping us avoid situations that may expose our core beliefs or by ensuring that any emotional pain we experience if they are exposed is minimized. This is where psychological needs and self-elements come into play. Psychological needs include the need not to have this core belief exposed. We may then develop a rule regarding how certain self-elements should look to meet this need.

For example, if someone believed they were incompetent, they might have a rule that "I must succeed academically" or

"I must always complete tasks to a high standard". These rules would then naturally increase the extent to which they identify with their education or career self-elements. Sometimes, rules are expressed as assumptions, such as, "If I don't pass my exams, others will see I'm incompetent". Because rules are linked to self-elements, threats to these will be perceived as having the potential to expose core beliefs and this will cause anxiety.

Whenever we encounter a situation that challenges one of our rules, negative thoughts are likely to arise linked to our underlying core beliefs. In CBT, these are called "negative automatic thoughts", and as the name suggests, they arise spontaneously into our conscious awareness. These thoughts might include things like, "I'm a *total* failure" and "*nobody* cares about me". You might recognize these thoughts as the kind of "thinking errors" we described in Chapter Five. Unfortunately, these serve only to reinforce our negative core beliefs, further undermining our self-perception while also strengthening our rules regarding our self-elements. This makes us vulnerable to experiencing more distressing thoughts when this rule is challenged again and is also likely to lead to unhelpful behaviours.

These behaviours are used to help us avoid our rules being broken as well as protect us in case they are. They include things like avoiding challenging tasks due to the belief that you'd be sure to fail or withdrawing socially because you believe that nobody really wants you there anyway. These behaviours may provide short-term relief but in the long run they'll worsen our self-perception and reinforce negative core beliefs. Avoidance fails to provide us with opportunities to challenge negative thinking patterns and correct the beliefs we hold about ourselves.

CBT works by helping us change our thinking patterns and behaviours, gradually reshaping our core beliefs and rules that keep us stuck. The result is improved self-perception and a reduction in symptoms of anxiety and depression. The good news is that the core skills taught in CBT are ones we can practise by ourselves. Let's take a look at them now, first focusing on our thinking or "cognition".

The Cognitive Approach

Two of CBT's most commonly used cognitive approaches are "cognitive restructuring" and "Socratic questioning". These techniques can help us challenge unhelpful and self-critical ways of thinking by examining and reframing our thoughts into more realistic, rational and kind ones. We can combine these techniques into a single exercise.

The first step is to identify an unhelpful thinking pattern that arises in response to a specific situation where you feel negatively toward yourself; either around your worth, ability or capacity to cope. These thinking patterns include the ones we described in Chapter Five, like "over-generalization", "fortune telling", "mental filtering", "catastrophization" and "personalization". Once we recognize that these are present, we can then practise the following:

Thought Reflection

1. Think of a recent situation where you experienced a negative internal dialogue about yourself. Often, these situations are associated with strong negative emotions, so it might be easiest to recall a time recently when you felt particularly sad, anxious or annoyed.
2. Write down the unhelpful thought you have identified, like "It's going to be a total disaster". This is an example of "catastrophization".
3. Underneath this thought, write down a brief explanation for why this thought arises. "I am having this thought because I am worried about . . . or because I feel that . . .". Can you

spot a rule that is being threatened or link it to a core belief? For example, the prediction that something is going to be a total disaster might be linked to the rule that "things must always turn out perfectly" and perhaps a core belief associated with being incompetent.

4. Now, examine this thought and challenge its validity. Ask yourself what evidence supports this thought? Is this thought always true? Is this thought based on facts or assumptions?

5. Next, ask yourself, "If the worst did happen, how could I cope?" or, "Even if this were true, what does it actually mean?" Is there a more balanced way you could view this situation? Write down an alternative thought, such as, "Maybe it won't go well, maybe it will. If it doesn't, it's not the end of the world and I'll just have to try something else".

The more we practise this, the easier it will be to identify our unhelpful ways of thinking and the more intuitive it will become to challenge our automatic negative thoughts. As you learn to better challenge your thoughts, you can also start to test out the validity of your underlying rules. Maybe you don't *always* have to do *everything* perfectly. Perhaps people won't think you're a *bad person* if you make mistakes. Over time, you will notice that the frequency of negative thinking will reduce, which will then have a positive knock-on effect on your self-perception.

The Behavioural Approach

Alongside changing the way we think, we can also look to replace behaviours that make us feel worse about ourselves with more helpful ones. The two most valuable behavioural interventions used in CBT are "activity scheduling" and "exposure therapy".

Activity scheduling is especially effective in treating depression. This is because the low self-worth that is felt in depression is often driven by our tendency to stop doing things. As we saw in Chapter Five, the less we do, the worse we feel. This is because isolating ourselves reinforces unhelpful beliefs like "I'm boring" or "I'm a waste of space" while also failing to provide experiences that counteract these ideas. If you find that you are stuck in this kind of depressive state, then I recommend practising the following:

Activity Scheduling

1. Write down a list of hobbies and activities you enjoyed before you felt down. They need not be anything arduous but ensure they are not unhelpful, for example going out drinking! Think about things that gave you a sense of achievement or pleasure.
2. Plan when and how often you will engage in each activity. Start with small, manageable tasks and gradually build up to more challenging ones. The key is consistency and having a balance of daily activities that include work, leisure and social activity. For example, perhaps you you've stopped spending time with friends. It may feel too much to organize a large get-together. However, meeting one of your close friends or organizing a phone call may feel manageable. The trick is to start small and slowly build it up.
3. Assess how you feel before and after each activity. Notice any changes in your mood or thoughts. Reflect on whether certain activities are more helpful than others and why that might be. It's often helpful to write these observations down in a journal alongside the activity.
4. Based on your reflections and evaluations, adjust your activity schedule. This may involve changing the frequency, time or type of activities to better suit your needs and

interests. It's normal to find this process difficult at first and you may feel tired after certain activities. This is to be expected, especially if you've been inactive for quite a long time.

5. Make sure you actively seek out and include social activities in your schedule. Interacting with others can provide support, increase feelings of belonging and help challenge negative thoughts about ourselves. It's normal to feel low motivation when we're depressed. This gives us the impression that doing things and seeing people is too much effort. However, activity actually energizes us when we're down. Try to recognize the low motivation as part of being depressed that needs to be overcome rather than as a reason why you shouldn't do something.

Like all of these techniques, the more you practise them, the easier they become. When it comes to low mood, "doing" is often the hardest but the most helpful thing. Remember that even if you don't *want* to do something, it doesn't mean that you can't. To get ourselves out of a depressive slump, we sometimes need to be strict on ourselves to be kind!

Exposure therapy is the favoured approach when our anxiety about an object, activity or situation leads to avoidance. For example, we may worry about taking the bus because it makes us feel claustrophobic. We then avoid taking the bus whenever possible. This may reduce our anxiety in the short term but over time it reinforces our fear because we begin to overestimate the level of threat and underestimate our ability to cope with it. Avoidance worsens our anxiety by triggering negative thinking that in turn activates our core beliefs and undermines our self-perception, particularly self-assurance.

Avoidance has its biggest impact when our fears are directly at odds with our daily lives and responsibilities. Imagine someone who feels anxious speaking in front of a group. Perhaps they are worried about saying something stupid or being asked a question they don't know the answer to. They may start avoiding certain meetings where they feel they might be exposed. Initially this helps them cope but soon they find they struggle in other meetings as well and may even find social gatherings intimidating. Before long they start doing whatever they can to avoid being around others, at work and socially.

If this person were to undergo CBT therapy, they would be recommended to implement exposure experiments. The Exposure Ladder, outlined below, is one such method for helping us overcome avoidance.

The Exposure Ladder

1. Identify the object, activity or situation that triggers your anxiety and leads to you avoiding something that would be helpful in your life. Don't choose something that should be avoided!

2. What is it about this object/activity/situation that makes you worried? What do you fear happening? What would be the consequence of this? You can use the techniques described in the thought reflection exercise earlier to examine the nature of your fear. Where possible, try to identify any unhelpful rules or core beliefs linked with your avoidant behaviour.

3. Make a list of situations that trigger your anxiety related to this fear, ranking them from most to least anxiety-provoking. Start with the situation that causes the most anxiety at the top and work down to the least anxiety-inducing situation. For example, if your fear is public speaking, you might put "giving a presentation in person to a large group of coworkers" at the top. This represents the most anxiety-provoking scenario. At the bottom, you might list "attending an online meeting with your camera and microphone off", as this is the least anxiety-inducing. Between these extremes,

include various situations that progressively increase your anxiety level as you move up the list.

4. This list then acts as your exposure ladder, which you gradually climb until you can face your worst fear without overwhelming anxiety. The word "gradually" is crucial. Only move to the next exposure level once you feel able to cope with the situation you are in with manageable levels of anxiety. As you climb the ladder, your self-assurance will grow as you become less avoidant.

5. At each stage of the process, reflect on how you are feeling and the thoughts you're having. What did you learn? How did it feel compared to what you expected? Were there moments where you felt more or less anxious? Use this information to adjust your approach, either by spending more time at the current stage or by making the next step less challenging if needed. Identify any unhelpful thoughts as they arise and apply the thought reflection technique to them.

Exposure therapy, behavioural activation and the restructuring of unhelpful thinking patterns, rules and beliefs are the central pillars of CBT and constitute the main treatment approaches for a variety of anxiety disorders and depression. If you find yourself experiencing high levels of distress and think these approaches may be helpful for you, I recommend looking into CBT in more detail. Research shows it can be effective even when done as self-help, i.e. without the help of a therapist. This could allow you to save money and avoid lengthy waiting lists for therapy!

The Art of Therapy

CBT is one of hundreds of psychotherapeutic approaches practised worldwide. Many of these approaches are different in terms of techniques they use and the psychological models they are based on. Most are delivered face-to-face over a period of months and all are generally trying to achieve the same outcome for their clients – improving how someone feels about themselves.

Given the sheer number of different therapies, we must ask ourselves how contrasting methods can produce similar outcomes. There must be a common quality that unites them – something that is always present, regardless of what approach is used. To see what this secret ingredient is, I want to introduce you to one of the most esteemed and influential figures in psychology, Carl Rogers.

Rogers is best known for his person-centred psychotherapeutic approach, which revolutionized the field of therapy. In his ground-breaking book, *On Becoming a Person*, Rogers says: "If I can provide a certain type of relationship, the other person will discover within himself the capacity to use that relationship for growth, and change and personal development will occur". Rogers identified that it is the therapeutic relationship between us and our therapists that holds the key to success in therapy. Specifically, Rogers argued that this relationship relies on therapists demonstrating three qualities – *authenticity* in how they respond to us, unconditional *acceptance* or "positive regard" toward us and a continuous desire to understand and *empathize* with our thoughts and feelings.

Rogers' perspective on therapy was significantly different from many of the beliefs that traditional psychologists and therapists held. Rogers saw therapy less as an intellectual exercise in problem-solving but more as a process of human relations. This perspective made therapy appear less governed by complex theories and textbook definitions and more dependent on interpersonal factors. Today, research supports Rogers' ideas regarding the importance of the therapeutic relationship. In the last few decades, studies have attempted to identify the most important elements of this relationship. One such study by Norcross and Lambert (2018) supports Rogers' hypothesis, finding positive regard and empathy to be "demonstrably effective" in the therapeutic relationship[6].

The Therapeutic Alliance

Interestingly, where I have proposed that human suffering is caused by a single problem – self-obsession, Rogers also believed that there is one problem at the root of our psychological pain. In his book, he describes this problem as a question all of us are asking: "Who am I, *really?* How can I get in touch with this real self, underlying all my surface behaviour? How can I become myself?"

When Rogers uses "self" he is referring to what I have described as our Person. In other words, I would be asking, how can I become the real Tom that is present underneath the version of myself I am currently presenting? While Rogers, like most psychologists, believed that we *are* our Person, he nevertheless recognized that central to our psychological distress is the disparity between our Person as it *is* (in his words, the "real self") and the Person we believe we *should* be. He described this inauthentic version of ourselves as a "false face" or "mask" that we feel we must "present to the world". These ideas align closely with what I discussed regarding the disparity that arises between how we perceive our self-elements and how we think they should be.

Rogers believed that therapeutic success occurs when we are able to drop the façade of who we think we should be and start being who we actually are. From Rogers' perspective, this is our Person as it is today rather than the Person we hope to become. This process of letting go of who we're not and becoming who we are is best described as self-acceptance (albeit Person-acceptance!). If therapists can create an unconditionally accepting and empathetic relationship with us, we'll naturally begin to internalize this acceptance and empathy. In effect, the acceptance and empathy that define the therapeutic relationship give rise to self-acceptance and self-compassion. It is these that are crucial to the success of therapy. As we will see, these same principles can be applied to ourselves, even without the help of a therapist.

The Elusiveness of Self-Acceptance

In self-acceptance, we change our deeply held beliefs about our Person and the self-elements we identify with. Specifically, we begin to see the self-elements we have and dislike through less critical eyes while also seeing those we don't have and wish we did as less critical determinants of who we are. In effect, we learn to let go of "what should be" and start to feel comfortable with "what is".

Therapy can help us develop self-acceptance but it is not the only way. Rogers also believed that the same principles underpinning an effective therapist-patient relationship can make other relationships equally therapeutic. This means we can improve our self-perception by surrounding ourselves with people who show us unconditional positive regard, whether that be family, friends or partners. Equally, we can boost the self-perception of those around us by radiating genuine warmth and acceptance toward them. In effect, our loved ones are our greatest therapists by virtue of simply being kind and loving us for who we are. It is an effortless therapeutic touch that we all possess by virtue of being human.

Self-acceptance is not dependent on others – it is something we can actively cultivate in ourselves. However, it has to be done in a slightly roundabout way, as the following example illustrates.

Imagine somebody who is unhappy because of awkwardness they feel in social situations. Perhaps they have always been a shy person, even as a child. Maybe this aspect of their self (their personality) has been something they have struggled to accept. They may have spent much of their life desperately trying to be the confident, outgoing person they feel they should be. If we were to tell this person, "Just accept you're shy", it probably wouldn't be of much help! After all, how can anyone accept something they fundamentally don't believe is true?

116

The only way we can accept something is to change the way we see it, that is to change our beliefs. In this example, it means learning that being shy is okay. If we can see that it is okay to be shy, we'll not have any difficulty accepting that shyness is part of who we are. Acceptance happens automatically once our negative judgement of something becomes neutral or positive. Ironically, once a person feels like it is okay to be shy, they will naturally become more confident. In other words, acceptance paradoxically leads to change.

This idea is at odds with what we often encounter in our everyday lives. For example, imagine I believed that I should be more spontaneous. If I expressed this desire to my friends, they might say, "Spontaneity is a great quality! This is something you should definitely work on". It is generally seen in our culture as something good, whereas being more of a planner is often regarded as being dull or unadventurous. Therefore, our friends might support the idea that we shouldn't accept that we're not naturally spontaneous. In other words, we are actively encouraged to try to change who we are.

Sometimes, this encouragement comes from those closest to us, people we respect the most. When a father tells his son he mustn't be so sensitive, this can shape a child's core beliefs about which traits are and are not acceptable. This child may then grow up never being able to come to terms with his sensitive side. This would cause low self-perception, expressed as either low self-worth or low self-assurance and may activate the self-obsession cycle, resulting in depression or anxiety later in life.

Learning to accept something about ourselves we don't like can be incredibly challenging. Such beliefs tend to be deep-rooted and they may have been reinforced for many years by our experiences as well as feedback from ourselves and others. Therefore self-acceptance is best achieved indirectly through self-compassion.

The Power of Self-Compassion

Being self-compassionate means believing you don't deserve to suffer. It means deepening your understanding that you, like everybody else, deserve peace and happiness. With self-compassion, you learn to see yourself through kind eyes rather than the hypercritical lenses that many people habitually use. Self-acceptance is the natural product of self-compassion.

To help foster self-compassion, we can use an effective technique called common humanity. Here's how you do it:

Practising Common Humanity

1. Find a moment to reflect on a recent time when you had a self-critical thought. It could be something like, "I *always* screw things up".
2. Think about this thought and try to find the underlying self-element or aspect of yourself that it relates to. For example, maybe you think you always mess things up because you're a clumsy person. This is the part of your self that you do not accept.
3. The next step is to consider how other people in the world, perhaps even people you know and love, may also have the same perceived flaw. Using the example above, this might mean imagining someone else who is also quite clumsy.
4. With a person (real or imaginary) in mind, allow natural feelings of compassion towards this individual to arise. It is easier to do this by thinking about someone you like!
5. As feelings of compassion grow, try to feel what it is like to care deeply about this other person. The longer you can remain with these feelings, the better.
6. Now, turn your attention back to yourself. Allow yourself to appreciate how the aspects you recognize in yourself are also

present in other people. Notice how our human experience is shared by millions of others.

7. With this recognition of shared humanity, allow the compassion you experienced for another to wash over you. You are also human and deserving of this compassion.

This technique can be practised anywhere and at any time. You will likely find that compassion comes more easily toward others than yourself, which is to be expected! However, with practice, the compassion you feel toward yourself will deepen. Over time, you'll begin to cultivate genuine self-compassion. With this self-compassion comes gradual self-acceptance. With self-acceptance, you'll notice you have fewer self-critical thoughts and your self-perception will improve.

To enhance the practice of common humanity, you can also incorporate positive reflection. This is often best done as a journalling exercise just before bed. Simply reflect on your day and write down any situations where you demonstrated kindness to those around you. Try to identify how your character traits positively impacted those around you. It might look something like this:

> Today, I helped a colleague with a task they were struggling with. I was empathic and I used my sense of humour to lighten the situation.
> When I am struggling, I also deserve help.

The more you can make being kind to yourself habitual, the more you will find that self-compassion arises spontaneously. With practice, you will gradually change the negative self-beliefs that undermine your self-perception.

Balancing Acceptance With Action

When we practise self-acceptance, it is important we are mindful of applying this technique in a way that is in our best interests. Self-acceptance doesn't mean non-action. It doesn't mean we should roll over and accept whatever life throws at us. This is particularly important in relation to some of our external self-elements, such as our career. For example, perhaps we have a colleague at work who is verbally abusive to us. We may feel afraid to speak to them. This fear is reasonable and an important indicator that their behaviour is unacceptable. Similarly, your instinct to avoid this person is also in your best interests. In this context, acceptance is to accept the present reality as it actually is. If the present reality is that our colleague is a bully, accepting this should lead us to make positive changes to improve our work situation. In other words, acceptance allows us to tackle problems as they arise in a self-compassionate way. This will protect us from a great deal of hurt in the medium to long term while helping us make sensible decisions.

Of course, many aspects of our lives are beyond our control. Distinguishing what we can and cannot influence is an important skill we must all learn. For example, it may be that the unhappiness we feel in our job is due to factors that we cannot change. In this situation, we may decide to change jobs. As we reflect on our lives, we will realize there are many more things we cannot control than things that we can. We must learn to accept this reality and ensure our energies are directed at things we can do something about. We must combine self-awareness with acceptance and skilful action.

To help put this into practice, we can use a tool called the decision tree. It is based on ideas from the book *Managing Your Mind* by psychologists Gillian Butler and Tony Hope. I have recreated the decision tree in a series of steps below.

The Decision Tree

1. Identify a situation that you feel unhappy with, perhaps a dilemma you're struggling to solve.

2. Determine whether it's something that you can do something about. Ask yourself, is it something under your control?
3. If you realize it is something that cannot be changed, then practise accepting the situation for what it is and see whether there is anything else that can be done. For example, could you make a different change that removes this current problem entirely? Sometimes there might be nothing that can be done. If this is the case, you must focus on accepting the situation for what it is. This might be achieved by practising the common humanity exercise described earlier in the chapter.
4. If it is something you can directly change, ask yourself whether anything can be done now.
5. If it is something you can change but not now, shift your focus to other things to limit unnecessary worry. If it can be resolved now, take concrete steps to make immediate changes. Once you have done what you can do now, shift your attention to other things.

When applying this framework to ourselves, we must ensure we apply it compassionately and wisely. For example, it is not a method we should apply to a character trait we dislike, such as shyness. As we have seen, self-acceptance is the approach needed there. We must also be mindful when we want to make changes to our physical bodies. Sometimes it is beneficial to work on ways to lose weight and become healthier. However, we must apply careful thought to determine whether we see things in a realistic, compassionate and helpful way. Would a change *really* be in our best interests? If used appropriately, the decision tree can be a valuable tool in helping us to distinguish the things we can change from the things we cannot.

Closing Thoughts

Improving our self-perception will undoubtedly reduce our psychological distress. This is why psychological therapies continue to help so many people worldwide. When it comes to the self-obsession cycle, traditional Western psychological approaches are well placed to tackle its key drivers. This is unsurprising since the cycle is, in many ways, a product of the traditional Western way of living. We have found a solution for a problem largely of our own making!

However, the self-obsession cycle does not begin with low self-perception. Instead, it starts with our identification with self-elements. To further slow the self-obsession cycle, we must learn to reduce our attachment to the self. To achieve this, we will next turn our attention to teachings found in Eastern philosophies.

REFLECTION

A few years ago I was seeing a Jungian therapist or analyst as they often call themselves. At the time I was faced with an existential dilemma that pulled me in opposite directions. I could see that clinging to my identity was keeping me trapped and yet I couldn't let this Person go. I wanted the best of both. I wanted to be free but I wanted to bring my Person with me.

Should I embrace my Person or leave him behind?

Some months later, cooking dinner, a question popped into my head and I burst out laughing:

Why don't I just do both?

"*When I let go of what I am, I become what I might be.*"

Laozi

LETTING GO OF YOUR SELF

Perhaps the most irritating advice I commonly receive before an important exam or interview is, "Don't be nervous". It's the kind of comment that makes me irrationally annoyed. "Oh, I don't have to be nervous? Guess I won't be then, thanks." Hopefully, you picked up on my sarcasm! Clearly, I don't *choose* to be nervous, and I can't *choose* not to be. If it was up to me, I would obviously choose to be totally self-assured and calm in any situation.

And just like we can't choose whether or not to be anxious, we also can't simply choose to let go of the self. In fact, being told to "Just let it go" might be even more annoying than "Don't be nervous"! How can we possibly let something go that we can't let go of? It's like telling someone not to feel hungry or to stop hiccupping. When it comes to self-elements, we can only let them go if we stop being attached to them. Imagine you have a ball superglued to your hand. You will only be able to drop the ball if we dissolve the glue. Then the ball will fall to the floor. There is no letting go involved since letting go is not an active process. This is the approach we must take with our self-elements. We must dissolve the glue that keeps us attached to them.

So, what is the glue? To put it bluntly, the glue is our ignorance. It is our well-meaning misjudgement of reality.

You might be thinking, "First, he called me self-obsessed and now he's calling me ignorant!" I am! You are! But please don't take it personally. You share your ignorance with almost everyone else on the planet. Most of us have grown up in a culture where self-obsession is normal and, more often than not, actively encouraged. As such, being called ambitious, high-achieving or driven tends to feel more like a compliment than an insult. We learn we should chase status and material possessions and cling to things we value. We come to believe that purpose comes from striving and we shouldn't be content with what we have and who we are. Self-obsession permeates every aspect of society like a highly contagious virus. But because this virus causes the same symptoms in all of us, we assume the symptoms are a normal part of the human experience. We are accustomed to feeling stressed and discontented and assign these feelings to the human condition and often see them as signs to double down or push on even harder. We tell ourselves the only way is through and see our discomfort as a sign we don't have enough or aren't yet the person we should be. As our stress and apathy turn into anxiety disorders and depression, we're perplexed as to why we should be feeling this way. We have, in effect, become so self-obsessed that we are unaware of our own self-obsession. This is ignorance on a monumental scale.

The real shame is that this issue has been recognized for at least 2,000 years, yet humankind's self-obsession has largely caused it to be ignored. The ultimate truth, which guides us to a state beyond self-obsession, is embedded in various philosophical traditions, particularly in the Eastern teachings of Buddhism, Hinduism and Taoism. They were long regarded as at odds with traditional Christian ideas and seen as mystical or esoteric, and the West largely discounted them. It's only been in the last century that Westerners have started to realize the timeless wisdom found in these misunderstood and underappreciated teachings. It is these teachings we will explore in this chapter.

Although I have called them teachings, they may best be thought of as truths about the nature of things. While these are truths we can grasp intellectually, they are only fully understood when experienced directly. This is critical if we are to change our deeply held beliefs. To do this, we must learn to practise something called self-inquiry.

Self-Inquiry

Self-inquiry is a method of deep introspection which allows us to explore our true nature and gain first-hand experience of the truths about the self. It is best done in meditation because this provides the stillness and focus needed. It allows us to detach from the constant chatter of our thoughts so our awareness can be unobstructed. If the term meditation feels intimidating, think of it as a form of deep relaxation which maintains conscious awareness.

Meditation is a skill, which means it takes practice. Our minds are used to being busy. We have a tendency to focus on whatever thoughts or images our minds generate. However, in meditation, our focus is on what happens in between these cognitions, in the space between thoughts. This will be challenging at first but don't be discouraged as it is something everyone finds difficult. It is normal for our attention to become caught up in our thoughts. With practice, you will find that these thoughts arise less frequently and a greater proportion of your time will be spent in pure awareness.

You may find initially that you can only meditate for a couple of minutes. This is a great start! With time and practice, you will be able to meditate comfortably for longer periods.

Meditation

1. Find a quiet place where you will not be disturbed.
2. Set yourself a five- or ten-minute timer (start short).

3. Make yourself comfortable, either sat on the floor or in a chair. Some people prefer to lie down but there is a risk of falling asleep!
4. Either close your eyes or keep them open with a soft focus on a point in front of you.
5. Take a few deep breaths to relax your body.
6. Focus your attention on your breathing.
7. As you become aware of intruding thoughts and sounds, acknowledge them without judgement and gently return your focus to the breath.
8. Stay open and relaxed. Do not strain to focus. Simply let thoughts come and go like leaves floating past on a river.

That's all there is to it! This is the basic technique we will use to practice self-inquiry. This technique is a powerful tool for overcoming self-obsession because every time you find the stillness between thoughts, you are free, whether that be for a fleeting second or a few minutes.

If you find the breath an unhelpful point of focus, try focusing on silence. This may sound a little strange. However, if you sit quietly and listen, you will notice a background hum that we tend to associate with silence. This can serve as a resting point for your awareness to return to whenever you notice your mind has drifted elsewhere. Interestingly, this sound associated with silence illustrates that silence itself is not nothingness like we think it is. While listening to the silence, you will find that noises come and go but the silence always remains detectable.

If you make meditation a part of your everyday routine, you will soon find you can sit comfortably for twenty or thirty minutes. Find a time each day when you will not be disturbed and commit to daily practice. The more of a routine it becomes, the better. Before long, meditation will become intuitive. Soon, you will want to do it and look forward to this part of your day. You will see first-hand the benefits of meditation on your mental well being, clarity of mind and inner peace. Sitting comfortably for twenty minutes is a sign you have developed the concentration needed to incorporate self-inquiry into some of your meditation sessions.

As we discuss the philosophical truths related to the self, I will add a ninth and tenth step of self-inquiry to this meditation. I strongly recommend you practise this basic meditation for a few weeks until you can sit comfortably for around fifteen minutes.

With that said, let's take a look at our first philosophical truth about the self.

Truth One: The Self is Empty

Everything in the world is made up of more than one thing. This is true of every animal, vegetable and mineral. You cannot find anything that is not compounded. This is the nature of all things, from planets to subatomic particles. All the phenomena we observe in the world around us appear when the things that make them are present and when causes and conditions are right. When causes and conditions change, phenomena will change, too. This is the nature of reality and is probably consistent with how you see things. However, if we dig a little deeper, we'll find more is going on than first meets the eye.

Imagine we disassembled a car into its individual parts and laid them out on the ground. If I picked up a screw and asked you whether this was the car, you'd say no. Regardless of what piece I picked up, you'd confidently tell me it was definitely not the car. Yet, if we put all these pieces back together again, the car would miraculously reappear. When the causes and conditions are right, the car appears. When the causes and conditions are not right, the car does not appear. This is the nature of all things. And like all things, when we look at the various materials that a car is made out of, we will not find the car. This is because a car is made only of non-car elements. There is nothing "car" actually in a car. The only thing "car" about it is how we see it and how we describe it.

The fact a car is made only of non-car elements means that a car does not exist independently. It is totally dependent on all the various non-car elements coming together correctly. This dependent origination is often referred to in Buddhism as emptiness. The car is empty of car, empty of independent existence. The word empty can often make us think of nothingness but this is not the case here. To be empty is to be empty of *something*. It does not mean that it has to be empty of everything. For example, take a glass of water. If you drink the water, the glass becomes empty of water. This does not mean what you hold in your hand is nothingness. Similarly, while a car is empty of car, it is not nothingness. The car is made up of many non-car elements.

We can apply the same logic to our physical bodies. The physical entity I think of as Tom is made of all non-Tom elements. It is empty of Tom but *full* of trillions of cells made up of non-cell elements. Within each cell, there are atoms created from the stars and supernovae of distant galaxies. Yet the cell, or indeed Tom, won't be anywhere to be seen. This is not just true of our physical body self-element but for each of our internal and external self-elements. For example, if you examine your career, you will find that it is composed of many non-career elements, including salary, working environments and specific responsibilities, as well as yourself and your colleagues. None of these things is the career itself because a career is empty of independent existence, just like a car and our physical bodies.

Looking beyond names and labels, everything is interdependent. Nothing exists in isolation. Everything is empty of itself but also full of the entire cosmos. We are not separate from the world around us. We are the world around us. Whenever we see ourselves as independent entities, we make a misperception. It is a misperception of duality where we separate the subject (us) from the object (the world around us). In actuality, everything is part of the same non-dualistic reality.

Meditating on Emptiness

The truth that all things are empty gives us our first focus for
self-inquiry. Once you are in a meditative state (step eight),
we can move to step nine. Ask yourself the following question:
"What are the causes of . . . ?"

For this gap, you can choose any object, such as a tree,
car or pencil. Simply ask yourself what is necessary for this
thing to exist as we see it, and notice that none of these
things are itself. Recognize that none of these things are
themselves uncompounded and depend on other causes
and conditions.

Once you have intellectually understood that the object
is indeed empty, move your attention to the self and do the
same with a self-element (step ten). Choose an external self-
element such as your body, job or relationship, as these are
often the easiest to visualize in the mind's eye. Then follow
the same thought process.

For example, if you choose to focus on your relationship
with your partner, think about the components that come
together in order for this relationship to exist. This would
include your partner and the causes and conditions necessary
for your partner to exist and for the two of you to have met.
Think about all the various events that had to occur in order
for you and your partner to end up standing face-to-face in the
same place at the same time.

As you examine your relationship, you will see that it
is empty of inherent existence and made up only of non-
relationship elements. "Relationship" is simply a name we
use to describe a complex web of causality. Just like the car
contains nothing "car", our relationship contains nothing
"relationship". Furthermore, all the things that make up our
relationship are themselves compounded and empty. Not
empty of nothing but empty of themselves.

As you come to the intellectual understanding that this
self-element is indeed empty, allow this understanding of

emptiness to spread to the whole self. Know that the self is empty and rest with this reality. Instead of *thinking* about this truth, let it wash over you as a *feeling* of emptiness.

With practice, you will directly experience the emptiness of all things in a similar way that you sense the humidity in the air or another person standing next to you.

Truth Two: The Self is One

We already know that a change in one self-element will invariably affect others. Whether that is our beliefs shaping what we study at university or our hobbies influencing who we want to date, no self-element exists independently. Causes and conditions that shape one self-element are also critical to others. It is similar to the idea that the same materials used to make a car can also be used to make a computer, bike or house. These materials are used simultaneously, acting as causes and conditions for multiple aspects of the self.

Whenever we find ourselves thinking about self-elements existing separately, we have fallen into the trap of duality. Self-elements are to the self what clouds are to the sky. Just as it would be wrong to point to the cloud and say that it isn't part of the sky, it would also be a mistake to think of a self-element as disconnected from other self-elements. The clouds are as much a part of the sky as the sky is part of the clouds. There is a non-dualistic relationship between all phenomena since all arise interdependently.

The more we see self-elements as interconnected, the less we will obsess over specific self-elements. We'll also start to see the self as continuous with the world around us, helping to erode the distinction between "you" and "me". This will foster deeper compassion and empathy through a less self-centric lens.

Meditating on Oneness

An understanding of interconnectedness and non-duality can be incorporated into meditation. Once in a meditative state (step eight), we can move to step nine. Ask yourself the following question: "How is this [choose an object] connected to all things?" Think about how its causes and conditions are also necessary for other objects. Appreciate that this object does not and cannot exist in isolation. Are there other objects or phenomena that depend on this object?

With the intellectual understanding that it does not exist separately from other things, switch your attention to a self-element (step ten) and ask yourself, "How is my [choose self-element] connected to my other self-elements and the world around me?" Let the feeling of interconnectedness spread to the whole self and all things. In time, you will begin to experience a sense of non-duality, like when you look at your hand and feel that it is part of your body.

Truth Three: The Self is Impermanent

All things that are compounded are in constant flux. Since everything is compounded, everything is changing all the time. This impermanence is fundamental to our existence and we often do not appreciate it. Impermanence means seasons change and night becomes day. Impermanence allows a seed to grow into a tree and a baby to become a child. It is the emptiness of all phenomena that allows these changes to happen. Emptiness makes life possible, including everything we know and love. If things were independent and fixed, they would never change. This means we could never come out of depression or overcome anxiety. Emptiness gives us hope because it means feelings of despair and grief will always improve.

If we consider our self-elements, change means that the things we have and do not like will also change. As will our perspectives on them. Similarly, self-elements we do not have but want may one day be part of our lives or become things we no longer want. As we look past duality, the divide between what we have and do not have will become less defined. With the distinction between self and non-self slowly dissolving, our self-perception will naturally improve since beliefs around "not being good enough" or "not having enough" will weaken.

But what about self-elements we do like? Does impermanence mean these things will change too? Yes, it does. All things will change, including things in your life you value and identify with most. All of the things you love are only present now because of impermanence. Emptiness allowed your partner to be born and find their way into your life. Impermanence allowed the embryo to become your baby. Impermanence meant you could learn and gain your education to secure the job you have. We cannot have it both ways. Impermanence cannot be switched on and off whenever you want. One day, the things you care about will be gone and someday so will you. This is life and something we all know, even if we prefer to pretend that this is not the case. However, this understanding need not make life any less enjoyable. Appreciating impermanence can make life more joyful.

If we understand impermanence, we will be more present and appreciate every moment that we can spend with the people we love or doing the things we enjoy. Understanding emptiness allows us to live life fully, taking nothing for granted. When things change and change they will we are prepared because we already know that what we value slips through our fingers. We know we cannot stop change. We need not cling to things we have because these things are not really ours to cling to. In any case, it does not matter how hard we grasp them, change is beyond our control.

Impermanence is a gift that can help us overcome self-obsession. The more we appreciate the changing nature of each self-element, the less we'll identify with them and the more we'll accept what is. The self is like water. We cannot hope to hold it in our bare hands. It is better to stretch out our palms and let the water wash over us.

Meditating on "Impermanence"

We can incorporate our understanding of impermanence into meditative practice. Once in a meditative state (step eight) ask yourself, "What had to change for this [choose an object] to exist?". You might want to think about the materials it is made out of and what had to happen for the object to exist in the form you recognize today. With the intellectual understanding that change was necessary in the formation of this object, switch your attention to a self-element (step nine) and consider, "How is my [self-element] also dependent on change?" For example, you may consider your career and the changes that had to happen for you to end up in the position you are currently in, in terms of personal development but also external factors beyond your control. Appreciate the impermanent nature of this self-element and allow the truth of impermanence to wash over the entire self. Know that all things are impermanent. Begin to feel the sense of freedom that impermanence provides.

Truth 4: The Self is Neither Good nor Bad

Imagine two people working for the same company doing the same role. Each has the same level of responsibility and similar workloads. One feels their job is relatively straightforward and they experience low levels of stress. However, the other person finds work incredibly stressful and spends much of their time worrying about it. The first person describes their job as good, the second says it's awful. Who is right?

Instinctively, we would say both are. After all, our experiences are subjective, and what one person likes is not necessarily the same as what someone else likes. In reality, neither person is right. The job is neutral and any notions of good or bad come from each person's mind, not the job itself.

The same is true of all things. The universe does not have good or bad, right or wrong, positive or negative. Just as phenomena are empty of independent existence, they are also empty of these inherent qualities. The tendency to label things in this way arises from our dualistic thinking, where we mistakenly categorize the world into binary opposites. Our categorization is based on our experiences, beliefs and other factors influenced by society and culture. Understandably, this way of thinking leads to problems. When we encounter something "good", we tend to immediately grasp at it and want it for ourselves. Conversely, when we identify something as "bad", we tend to feel aversion and want to avoid it.

When it comes to self-elements, we have preconceived ideas regarding what we think is desirable and undesirable. This is what makes our brains evaluate ourselves positively or negatively. Where its judgement is positive, we experience attachment and clinging. When negative, we experience aversion and a desire for something other than what is. Our overall self-perception is created by our brains projecting value judgements onto fundamentally neutral self-elements.

If we approach self-elements with equanimity, we identify less with aspects of ourselves we once saw as inherently good or bad. We approach change with openness and curiosity. Rather than resisting change or wishing for it to happen, we can be more accepting of what is. A self-element that changes simply moves from one neutral state to another neutral state. We can be more mindful of positive and negative perceptions coming from our dualistic mindset. Instead of trying to control the uncontrollable, our focus will naturally turn to our thoughts and beliefs. It is here where we can truly alter our experience.

Of course, it is important to recognize that just because phenomena are empty of inherently good or bad properties, it doesn't mean it's *okay* to have an abusive partner or a boss who bullies you. Understanding this distinction is crucial for maintaining healthy boundaries and advocating for ourselves in hurtful situations. Appreciating that phenomena are inherently neutral does not equate to condoning unethical behaviour. It empowers us to respond to situations with self-compassion, freeing us from unhelpful beliefs that may keep us stuck in harm's way.

Meditating on Neutrality

Once you're in a meditative state (step eight), try to recall a situation that seemed bad at first but led to something more favourable (step nine). Perhaps it was an unexpected delay that turned out to be a blessing. Or a job interview rejection that paved the way to a role you preferred. Good and bad arise from your beliefs about situations and things rather than from the situations and things themselves. With this intellectual understanding, switch your attention to a self-element that you feel negatively toward (step ten) and ask yourself, "Is this aspect of myself bad or do I just believe it to be?" What would this aspect of your self look like if you were to apply objectivity? Allow the truth of neutrality to wash over the entire self. Know that all things are free from right and wrong. Feel the sense of freedom that non-duality provides.

The Four Truths

Changing how we see self-elements changes our relationship with them. The tendency we have to identify with the self is the direct consequence of the ignorant lens through which we see our selves and the world around us. As our perspective shifts, our self-obsession will lessen. As self-obsession fades, psychological pain will subside.

Here are the four truths regarding self-elements described in this chapter:

1. Every self-element is compounded (empty of independent existence).
2. All self-elements are interdependent.
3. All self-elements are impermanent.
4. No self-element is inherently good or bad.

Philosophical Inquiry

Alongside meditation and self-inquiry, we can practise philosophical inquiry in our everyday lives. This can be done anywhere and anytime since everything in our lives is empty of independent existence, just like us. I enjoy doing this exercise when I am out walking. I look around at plants or animals and think to myself, "What is a tree?" or "What is a bird?" I reflect on how impermanent the natural world is and how interconnected everything is. I remind myself that the names I use for things are simply names, beneath which is an infinitely complex web of causality. I then consider my place within this world and apply the same reasoning to myself.

Inquiry into our self and the things around us helps us overcome attachment and encourages us to see things for what they really are. The more we practise it, the more we will live our lives in accordance with reality.

Closing Thoughts

The way we see the self is critical to how we relate to it. Letting go of our attachment to self-elements reduces our vulnerability to their inherent instability. This represents a critical step in overcoming self-obsession since changing how we see the self will change the extent to which we identify with it.

Letting go is a gradual process. It involves a fundamental shift in our beliefs, which requires a combination of intellectual insight and lived experience. Through meditative and philosophical self-inquiry, we are able to replace ignorant beliefs and take the first steps toward freedom. The four truths described here represent four aspects of the non-dualistic nature of reality. It is a reality that has been known about for millennia and modern science is only now catching up.

Discoveries in quantum physics have begun to bring scientific backing to these long overlooked philosophical truths. For example, at the level of subatomic particles, the behaviour or characteristics of one particle can influence another instantaneously over vast distances in a way which suggests their states are inherently linked. This phenomenon is known as quantum entanglement and supports the idea that nothing can truly exist as an isolated and separate entity. Similarly, research in quantum physics has also found that particles can exist in multiple states or in multiple places simultaneously. The precise state or location of a particle can only be determined by the act of measuring it. At the quantum level, objective reality appears to be influenced by subjective observation. It is therefore impossible to separate the observer from the observed. This is known in quantum physics as the observer effect. I urge anyone who is interested in exploring this further to look up the famous double-slit experiment, which is truly mind-boggling. It reveals how individual particles can travel as waves of probability, with their exact location only determined upon observation. When a single photon of light, for example, is fired at a wall with two slits, it somehow travels through both openings and neither at the same time!

Ultimately, how we tend to see things is not how things truly are. As our understanding of quantum physics deepens, it is not too reductive to say that science is finding parallels with ancient wisdom found in Eastern philosophies. And yet this wisdom requires no scientific proof. It is simply a description of what you and I can see to be true in ourselves and the world around us. The biggest challenge comes from embracing this truth in the depths of our being and replacing misguided beliefs that we have clung to for so long.

REFLECTION

There is a Taoist parable called The Empty Boat. In this story, a man rows his boat along a river in dense fog. He rows slowly, careful not to hit any branches or strike the bank. Out of nowhere a boat emerges from the fog and collides with his own, causing him to tumble from his seat. Angry, he pulls himself up from the bottom of the boat, shouting at the other boatman to stay clear and watch where he's rowing. But as the boat passes, he sees it is empty, adrift on the current and his anger dissipates.

"A human being is a part of the whole called by us universe, a part limited in time and space. He experiences himself, his thoughts and feelings as something separated from the rest, a kind of optical delusion of his consciousness."

Albert Einstein

TOUCHING THE ULTIMATE

There is a famous story in Zen Buddhism that describes a series of exchanges between a student and a Zen master.

Determined to achieve enlightenment, a student approaches his master for advice. "I don't understand what I'm doing wrong," says the student. "I meditate every day. I've given up my treasured possessions. I've cut all social ties. I've followed the Buddhist path as it should be followed. And yet, enlightenment escapes me. Please, master, give me one piece of advice."

The master listens carefully before replying. "You have given up so much in the pursuit of enlightenment, but there's still one thing you must let go of."

"What is it, master? Please tell me! I have given up all my desires . . ."

The master smiled and simply said, "Give up your desire for enlightenment."

Imagine how perplexed this poor student would have been! How can you obtain something you don't want to obtain? It seems like impossible advice. Yet hidden within this paradox is a greater truth. There is *nothing* to obtain, and there is *nobody* to obtain it. The student was confused because he saw enlightenment as something separate from what he had, thus making the mistake of duality. The master reminded the student that enlightenment is already present, just like the sun is there before the clouds part and the stars are there before night falls.

The student's need for enlightenment was a need of their Person. It is only through the eyes of their Person that they have desires. To let go of all desires, they must let go of the Person who has desires. Beyond this Person is total freedom.

The term enlightenment is one which is thrown around carelessly and carries a lot of baggage. When I began to study Buddhist philosophy, I naturally bristled when I read the word enlightenment. I was a proud atheist and enlightenment seemed too religious and otherworldly for my liking. However, I've come to realize that enlightenment isn't weird at all. It's simply seeing things for what they are. It's stepping beyond the nonsensical way we think about ourselves and the Person we have convinced ourselves we are. Enlightenment is called awakening because it's a process of waking up to how things have always been. It's not something we follow with blind faith. It's something we can realize is true for ourselves. To do that, we must gradually let go of the Person who has caused us so much pain.

A Wave Called Tom

Imagine a wave, let's call it Tom. Imagine he was born from the ocean's depths and rose to the water's surface alongside other waves. As Tom travelled across the sea, he'd look behind at where he had been and ahead at where he was going. All around him were other waves of varying shapes and sizes, all moving in a similar direction. When Tom looked at other waves, he sometimes felt jealous of characteristics he didn't see in himself. If only he was taller or moved with the same grace and elegance.

Sometimes he encountered pieces of driftwood and other items carried in the current. He held onto them for as long as he could before they slipped from his embrace into the grateful arms of other waves. As he watched these treasured items slowly disappear into the vastness of the ocean, he felt a sense of loss. He wished he was strong enough to keep hold of things he valued.

When Tom looked ahead, he often felt afraid. He saw waves crashing on a distant shoreline and feared what would happen to him once he reached the shallow water. When the sky darkened overhead he worried about storms and how he'd cope if the weather turned.

As Tom travelled across the ocean, he often felt alone. A small wave lost in a sea of millions of others. He didn't understand why he was there or what any of it meant. He just knew that he was vulnerable to the tides and where the current and prevailing winds would take him. Often, the ocean didn't feel like home. Sometimes he wished he was never a wave at all.

The Wave is Free

How did you feel as you read the wave's story? Did it evoke feelings of sympathy toward the wave? Did you feel frustrated because his suffering seemed unnecessary? Maybe it felt like you were reading about your life. After all, this wave's journey is in many ways similar to our own and I didn't name it Tom by chance! This metaphor encapsulates the human condition and the challenges we encounter. When we listen to the wave's struggles, his pain seems reasonable. Of course he would feel afraid in such circumstances.

If you could speak this wave's language, perhaps you would try to make him feel better. You may begin by telling him that you understand what he's going through and why he feels how he does. This would make him feel less alone. You may then tell him not to worry because the fate of any wave is the same and thinking about it will make no difference. However, this may make the wave feel even more despair at the hopelessness of his situation. As we all know, there are few things less helpful than someone telling us "Not to worry" or saying that there are "Plenty more pieces of driftwood in the sea"! Even telling him that he is beautiful the way he is will be unlikely to change how he sees himself compared to others.

But there is one piece of advice that may change the wave's experience entirely. A single simple solution that will resolve this wave's difficulties.

"Remember, you are water."

The wave suffers because it sees itself as separate from the ocean. It forgets that it is itself the ocean. The wave and the ocean are two forms of the same thing. We do not think of a wave as being born because we know the water was there all along. Similarly when a wave breaks on the shoreline we do not describe it as dying. We know the water simply returns to the sea in a different form. There is no separation between one wave and another. All waves are the ocean.

Each wave is empty of independent existence. Each wave is connected to every other wave through the water it is made of. Each wave is impermanent as its causes and conditions are in constant flux. Once we look past the false separation between a wave and the sea, we'll see that the true nature of things is beyond duality, beyond notions of birth and death, good and bad, right and wrong. It does not matter how tall a wave is or what driftwood falls in its path. Nor does it matter what distance it travels or what shoreline it reaches. A wave is just a wave, water is just water.

We are all waves. The self-elements we identify with are the materials drifting on the surface of the water and the weather overhead. Like us, these things are also empty and impermanent. They are not ours and never will be, however much we cling to them.

To change our perspective on ourselves, we need to experience this reality for ourselves. A conceptual understanding is not enough. The truth is a practical truth, and, as such, we need to practise it.

Meditating on the Absolute

We have discussed meditation and self-inquiry. We must now extend this inquiry to include inquiry of our Person.

1. Once in a meditative state, focusing on either your breath or silence, shift your awareness inward to your conscious experience.
2. Ask yourself, "*Who* am I?"
3. As thoughts, feelings and sensations arise, observe them and ask yourself: "Whose thought is this?" "Who is feeling this?" "Who do these sensations belong to?"
4. Whenever you find your mind trying to answer these questions intellectually, shift your focus back to the question and feeling of "I" or "me".
5. Through continual practice, you may find moments where thoughts subside and the sense of "I" dissolves, leaving only awareness itself.
6. Rest in this awareness, trying not to conceptualize your experience with thoughts.

During self-inquiry, the aim is not to create or change any feelings or thoughts you have but to be aware of what is. The non-duality we experience is not something new to discover but something that has been here all along that we can learn to notice.

All Emotions are Empty

Inquiry into our Person also involves inquiry into our thoughts, feelings and emotions. We tend to regard these mental formulations as being part of who we are. We say things like "I feel sad" or "I am happy". This is similar to saying, "I am a teacher" or "I am tall". However, none of these things belong to anyone. Our Person is empty of independent existence and the "I" simply represents conscious awareness. In reality, there is nobody having these thoughts, no thinker of a thought or feeler of an emotion. These phenomena arise when causes and conditions are right and cease when causes and conditions change.

Our thoughts and feelings change like the weather. Just like the weather is not us, neither are our mental states. When it's sunny, we don't cling to the blue sky or push away clouds. When it rains, we don't stop water falling from the sky. We don't try to control the weather because we know it's not part of us. We also know the weather and seasons are impermanent. The rain eventually gives way to the sun and winter gives way to spring. We can never stop the changing seasons or affect the weather. All we can do is take whatever comes our way and make the most of the sun or ride out the rain.

But when we are happy, we cling to this feeling for as long as we can. We think happiness is something that is ours and something we can keep. Rather than simply enjoying it while it is here, we actively pursue it and attempt to destroy anything in its path. The pursuit of happiness leads to a continuous cycle of desire and dissatisfaction. We constantly seek it, but each time we touch it, we're powerless to stop it from slipping away. It is like when children play with bubble machines. Every time they catch a bubble, it vanishes. No matter how fast they run, how quickly they react, or how long they play, their hands will remain empty.

There is a Buddhist expression that translates to, "All emotions are painful". It is not just fear, despair and loss that cause us pain. Happiness, love and excitement hurt us too. This is because all emotions are inherently transient. Happiness will undoubtedly fade, love will become loss and excitement will diminish. Our attachment to these fleeting states and our desire to prolong them sets us up to suffer when they change.

But it is important to remember that just because emotions are associated with pain does not mean they are inherently negative phenomena. Pain arises not from the emotions themselves but from our resistance to them and their impermanence. Understanding the emptiness of emotion can help to change our relationship with self-elements and our Person. The things we value in our lives can never bring us lasting happiness. They can provide temporary pleasure before they inevitably change. Clinging to self-elements as a means of chasing happiness is a futile endeavour. True happiness is found not in the attachment to things but rather in the detachment from all things.

A River Crossing

There is a Zen Buddhist parable called The Two Monks and a Woman. In the story, two monks travel on foot to a nearby village. They belong to a school of Buddhism that strictly forbids physical contact with women. On their journey, they come to a shallow but fast-moving river. As they reach the water, they see a frail woman sitting on the bank crying. The younger of the monks asks her why she's upset. She replies that the current is too strong to cross the river to see her family. The older monk immediately scoops the woman up, carries her across the river and sets her down on the other side.

For the rest of the journey, the younger monk walks in stunned silence. He's consumed by thoughts about what's happened. He can't understand why his elder would break an important and sacred rule. Finally, unable to contain his confusion and frustration any longer, he blurts out,

"How could you carry that woman?!"

The older monk simply replies, "I left the woman back at the river. Why are *you* still carrying her?"

This story is a lesson in letting go of our mental attachments and judgements. It is our rigidly held beliefs and strong feelings that we stubbornly cling to which gives us so much pain. All our emotions are empty and are not ours to cling to.

Beyond Concept

When I describe freedom beyond our Person, it is important to reiterate that this is a freedom that can't be understood solely through intellectual understanding. Just like we can't learn to drive without sitting behind the wheel of a car, this freedom cannot be understood by reading a book. Enlightenment is beyond all knowledge and conceptual understanding. Our attachment to things will serve as a barrier to freedom. This was the message given by Buddha in the following teaching.

In the story, Buddha compares the Buddhist teachings (or dharma) to a raft. He explains that if a person needs to cross a dangerous river, they should build a raft to help them safely reach the other shore. But the Buddha then asks whether this person should carry their raft with them on their onward journey or leave it behind.

Buddha says they should leave the raft behind. Once the raft has taken them to the other shore, it has served its purpose and should not be held on to. In this analogy, the river represents the human condition, known as samsara in Buddhism. The other shore is freedom or nirvana. The teaching represented here is encapsulated in the raft that is only meant to take us to the shoreline of nirvana. Once we're there, we must experience it for ourselves.

This same sentiment is echoed in Zen Buddhism by the phrase, "The finger pointing at the moon is not the moon." In other words, the teachings (the finger) are not the ultimate truth or enlightenment (the moon) itself. To truly understand and experience enlightenment, one must look beyond the teachings and have a direct, personal experience of it (seeing the moon in all its splendour). This analogy reminds us that knowledge, while valuable, only points us toward a deeper truth which must be experienced to be fully understood.

Emptiness is not Nothingness

When I talk about moving beyond our Person or letting go of our Person, I'm not suggesting that everything that is Tom should cease to exist. A common misconception of Buddhist philosophy is that it is nihilistic. But this is to suggest there is nothingness, which is not the case. Our Person is not non-existent. It exists and we can describe it. However, we describe it as *empty* because it doesn't exist in the way we think it does. We describe *letting it go* because we must let go of our misguided beliefs about it. To be free is not to have no Person at all. It is simply to be free of that Person's desires and pain. This concept is beautifully described in a Buddhist teaching on emptiness.

One day, a student approached a renowned monk, expressing confusion about the concept of emptiness. He asked the monk, "If everything is empty, does this mean nothing exists? Is everything we see an illusion?"

The monk smiled and invited the student to sit with him. He picked up a cup and placed it on the table in front of them. "Is this cup real?" he asked the student.

"Of course, it's real! I can see and touch it."

The monk then picked up the cup and threw it on the floor. It smashed into hundreds of pieces. The student watched in surprise.

"Now," said the monk, "where's the cup?"

"It's no longer there, it's broken," the student replied in shock.

"No, the cup has changed form but the material it was made from still exists," explained the monk. "When we say things are empty, we mean they do not exist in isolation, independently or permanently. Emptiness is not nothingness, quite the opposite!"

The student's eyes widened as he understood the truth. As he got up to leave, he thanked the monk and said, "I'm sorry you had to break your cup."

"Oh, don't worry about that. It was already broken."

Closing Thoughts

If you let go of some of your self-elements, you will find some peace. If you let go of many self-elements, you will have much peace. If you can let go of your Person, you will have total freedom. Waiting for you on the other side is someone you know very well, but it's someone who has been obscured by your Person for many years. That someone is *you*. As you slowly break free from your self-obsessed cage, you'll find yourself waiting with open arms.

REFLECTION

Since discovering my love for walking, I have hiked almost 10,000 kilometres across the UK and Europe. I have mostly followed footpaths of the Camino de Santiago, a series of pilgrimage routes that end at the cathedral in Santiago de Compostela in northwest Spain.

The Camino has given me much. It was an escape from anxiety and a cure for panic attacks. A place of deep introspection when I grieved the loss of my career.

It was somewhere I went to "find myself" and experience freedom from the life I felt bound to. But the more I looked for Tom, the more I realized there was nobody to find. An increasingly aimless pursuit.

When I was walking to Santiago again last year it dawned on me I had nowhere to go and no reason to go there. My walk became effortless.

"Form is emptiness, emptiness is form. Emptiness is not separate from form, form is not separate from emptiness. Whatever is form is emptiness, whatever is emptiness is form."

Buddha

RETURNING TO YOUR SOURCE

Your Person exists within your conscious awareness. Your Person is not consciously aware. When I first became aware of this alternative way of seeing the human experience I was shocked because I knew it was right. At first, it made me feel disorientated like someone had woken me up from a dream. I also felt conflicted since I couldn't deny the truth of what I was reading and yet was unsure as to whether I was ready to let go of my Person. I could see sense in reducing my attachment to my self and improving my self-perception but letting go of my Person felt like a step too far. I didn't want to *not be* Tom. I just wanted to be a happier version of him.

This reluctance to let go is common and is a direct consequence of the conditioning our brains have received throughout our lives. It is incredibly hard for us to accept that our Person is part of our experience rather than the one who is doing the experiencing. Our brains don't want to let go of our Person and this attachment is strengthened by our habitual thinking and continuously reinforced by the self-obsessed societies in which we live. To help our minds let go of our Person, we must provide them with something else to hold on to, something tangible they can identify with.

Who We Really Are

Much of the wisdom I've described so far is associated with Buddhist teachings. However, such insights are not limited to Buddhism, a philosophy that originated in India around 2,500 years ago. Similar truths are present in other philosophical traditions and world religions. One such tradition is Taoism, which developed in China at a similar time as Buddhism was emerging in India. While the Buddhist teachings are largely attributed to Siddhartha Gautama, known as Buddha, Taoist teachings are traditionally attributed to Laozi (Lao Tzu). While Buddhism and Taoism are distinct in many ways, there are indisputable similarities and shared themes, especially in relation to topics such as meditation, the nature of reality and who we really are. It is the "who we are" that we will turn our attention to now.

I have discussed how every animal has its own nature and its own unique way of responding to the world. While I have called this their nature it is known by different names in different philosophies. In Buddhism, it is called Buddha nature, while in Taoism it is referred to as the Tao. In the latter, it is often described as the unnameable, which gives a clue as to its elusive qualities! While I think Buddhist teachings best describe the process of letting go of our self and Person, I believe Taoism provides us with the best guidance in terms of how to reconnect with our nature.

In the last chapter I introduced a metaphor of a wave emerging from the ocean. We saw how it's separated from the ocean only in name, as both are made of water. If we were to relate this analogy to Taoism, the ocean would be the Tao. The wave emerges from it and later returns to it. This is true of all phenomena. All emerge from the Tao and return to the Tao. However, since the wave and the ocean are both water, the wave is as much the Tao as the ocean. In fact, the driftwood and the weather are the Tao too. This is because the nature of reality is non-dualistic.

The Tao is everywhere and nowhere, found in everything and nothing. It is vanishingly small and infinitely vast. It is the source of all things and is also the things themselves. Through the Tao, everything is connected and all notions of separation fade away. The Tao can therefore be considered an expression of reality, perhaps similar to how physicists describe quantum matter or energy. And just like energy cannot be created or destroyed, the Tao is ever-present, simply changing form to manifest into the phenomena that makes up the world.

All things are expressions of the Tao, including you and me. It is the Tao that gives life inherent spontaneity and authenticity. In their natural state, all things align with the flow of the Tao, like streams flowing into a single mighty river. The Tao gives rise to the apparent order that we see in the natural world, allowing plants and animals to exist in balance and harmony. It is said that life in accordance with the Tao unfolds without force or interference. In other words, when things are true to their nature, life occurs effortlessly and with synchronicity.

In Taoism, the spiritual path is one of returning to our original source, our inner Tao, our nature. By realigning ourselves with our nature, we can live in a way that is true to ourselves rather than living as slaves to our Person. This natural state is sometimes compared to an uncarved block. It is our primitive state of being that we were born with before it was shaped by our attachment to our Person. The Taoist path can help us embrace our nature, allowing us to discover that the nobody that lies beyond our Person is who we really are. By returning to the Tao, or our uncarved block, we return to our unconditioned state at one with the rest of the universe.

To get there, we can draw on the wisdom of Laozi's great Taoist philosophical text, the Tao Te Ching[7]. I will present key themes alongside exercises you can practise to make the changes needed to live according to your nature.

Have but Don't Possess

It is not the things in our lives that cause us pain but the relationship we have with these things. Since everything changes, attachment to material possessions will always lead to dissatisfaction or loss. Nothing external can bring us everlasting joy and happiness. Contentment can only be found by living in accordance with our true nature. Here, there is nothing lacking and therefore no need to cling to things. Without anything to cling to, there's nothing to lose and you can free yourself from grief and desire. Things come and go, and you can enjoy them without resisting their departure. This same wisdom can be applied to aspects of your self which are as impermanent as material possessions. Can you learn to see your self objectively as an extension of your Person rather than an aspect of your nature? Can you free yourself from envy and greed?

"Once you know you have enough, the entire world is yours."
Laozi

Practicing Gratitude and Mindful Consumption

1. Begin your day with a moment of reflection. Write down three things that you have that you are grateful for. These may include things that help you meet your basic needs or items you enjoy. It could be anything from the radiators that keep you warm in winter to the cup of coffee that starts your day. Consider doing this as part of a gratitude meditation.

2. When you find yourself in a position to buy something new, remind yourself of things you already have that fulfil your needs. Ask yourself, "Do I really need this extra thing?" "How does this add value to my life?" "What are the impacts of this purchase on the environment and society?" Can you work toward a more minimalist way of living?

3. When you need to make a significant purchase, consider implementing a waiting period for things that are non-essential. Decide on a specific time frame, perhaps a few days, during which you'll mull over the potential purchase. This can help reduce impulse buying and ensures you only add things that truly contribute to your wellbeing. This is particularly helpful for those of us who browse online retailers!

4. Practise gratitude by journalling before bed. Reflect on your day and note the moments or people that brought you joy or contentment. Notice the abundance present in your life. What else do you actually need?

Be Wary of Ambition

Through our Person we continuously look to better our selves to meet our Person's evolving psychological needs. This includes our need for recognition, approval and status. In our nature, there's nothing that needs to be changed since we are exactly how we should be. When we live according to our nature everything we do succeeds since we are not striving for any state other than what already is. This is the joy of aimlessness. We have nothing we need to do and nowhere we need to go. It is said that a good traveller has flexible plans and no definitive destination. By returning to our nature, we free ourselves from the dualistic notions of success and failure. We become content with who we are. We let go of excessive pride and the need to compete with others. We stop comparing ourselves to those around us and overcome feelings of jealousy. Life becomes play since we are no longer attached to the outcome. We never expect success so are never disappointed. We are happy to *be* rather than *become.*

"If you stand on tiptoe, you will not stand firm." Laozi

Practising Tranquillity

1. Find a quiet place where you can sit comfortably without distractions. Spend a few moments calming your mind and relaxing your body. You may want to begin with a few minutes of meditation or breathing exercises.
2. Think back to a time when you felt truly happy and content. Not because of external achievements or recognition but because you were deeply engaged or at peace in the moment. It could have been taking a walk in nature or spending time with family or friends. These moments are often ones where you lose yourself and track of time, perhaps in a favourite hobby or creative activity.
3. Imagine yourself back in that situation. Focus on how it felt to be connected to your nature and free from the busyness of life.
4. What aspects of these experiences brought you joy? Perhaps it was the connection you felt to others, the beauty of nature or the absence of stress. Identifying what it is that brings you peace allows you to recognize which factors can help you align to your nature.
5. Based on your insights, plan how you can incorporate more of these joy-filled moments into your daily routine. Set intentions to do these things regularly. The goal is to enrich your life with experiences that resonate with your true nature.
6. Once you make it a regular practice, take time to assess the impact these activities have on your well-being. What else can you add? What activities might you remove?

Treat the World as Yourself

The illusion of being our Person can be described as the illusion of separation. In self-obsession, we wrongly assume there's a "me" and a "you" and that we are disconnected individuals. With a dualistic perspective we can find ourselves exploiting and disregarding other people as well as the planet because we see them as "other". In reality, beyond our Person, we are part of the same interconnected phenomenon that we call the universe or Taoists refer to as the Tao. In our true nature, there is no distinction between anybody. When we begin to realize this truth, we will become compassionate to everyone because their pain is our pain as well. This will lead to what Rogers referred to as unconditional positive regard and an intrinsic desire to help others. This is because helping others helps ourselves. If I am compassionate to you, then I am simultaneously practising self-compassion while also realigning myself with my nature.

"Be kind to the kind and kind to the unkind since kindness is your being." Laozi

Practicing Kindness

1. Begin with a quiet reflection on interconnectedness. Consider how your actions impact other people and how their actions affect you. Recognize that the separateness we feel is an illusion of duality. We are as much a part of the world as the world is part of us.
2. Set a goal to perform at least one act of kindness each day. This could be as simple as giving somebody a compliment or offering your seat to someone on the bus. It could also involve volunteering or donating to a cause that benefits your community.
3. At the end of each day reflect on any acts of kindness you have done. Notice how these actions made you feel and how they were received by others. Does practising kindness make you feel more connected to others and the world around you?
4. Extend kindness to people in your life whom you normally overlook or actively dislike. Observe how treating them with compassion affects your relationship with them and how being kind to those people you find challenging makes you feel. The more you practise kindness, the more effortless it will become.

Embrace Simplicity

The self-obsessed mind often believes a fulfilling life should be busy and full of things. However, this leads to a life cluttered with unnecessary burdens and stress. This makes us more self-obsessed and shifts our focus away from our nature. Living simply means reducing excess noise and focusing on what is essential. This means living in accordance with our nature, which is inherently uncomplicated. Here, our needs are easily met and we can find contentment in the present moment, freeing us from the relentless pursuit for more. When we are not caught up in the endless distractions and desires, we're able to connect more deeply with ourselves, others and the world around us.

"*Simplicity, patience, compassion. These are your greatest treasures.*" Laozi

Practicing Simplicity

1. Select a task you perform while multitasking. This could be eating, reading, spending time with a friend or even boiling the kettle.
2. Before doing this task, take steps to minimize distractions in your environment. This might include turning off your phone or clearing your workspace of unrelated things.
3. Set your intention to remain present and fully engaged with this one activity until it is complete. For example, say, "For the next ten minutes, I am only eating my dinner."
4. Now engage fully with the task. Be mindful of every aspect of the activity. Pay attention to any sounds, smells, tastes or other sensations you experience. Allow your focus to remain on the thing you're doing.
5. If distractions arise or you catch yourself starting to multi task, gently acknowledge it and bring your attention back to the single activity. This may happen repeatedly, which is normal!

6. Once you've completed the task, take a moment to reflect. Were you more efficient? Did you feel more relaxed? Did the task feel different to normal? The more you practise this exercise of single-tasking, the more easily you'll be able to keep your attention focused on one thing.

Live With Moderation

When we view the world through our Person, we can easily fall into the trap of seeing things in dualistic extremes. This perspective can lead to excessive behaviour, consumption, emotional responses, or ambition, creating imbalance and disharmony within ourselves and in the world around us. It often manifests as excessive worry. The more we try to do and control, the more things remain undone and the more uncontrollable life appears. It is important to know when to stop. Living in moderation helps us resist the temptations of self-obsession, keeping us grounded in our true nature and content with what is.

"Fill your bowl to the brim and it will spill. Keep sharpening your knife and it will blunt." Laozi

Practicing Moderation

1. Spend a day or two observing your daily habits. Make a note of any areas where you are overindulging in a manner that is unhealthy or unnecessary. For example, eating, working, spending or even worrying.
2. Choose one or two areas where you've noticed the most excess. Now, set specific and achievable targets to work toward to reduce these behaviours. For example, if you're overworking reduce working hours by a certain number each week or take longer lunch breaks.

3. For each goal implement practical strategies to encourage moderation. For example, set reminders on your phone, adhere to strict budgets or block out time in your calendar for self-care.
4. At the end of each week reflect on your efforts to live in moderation. Consider how the changes have made you feel then adjust your goals and strategies to make further progress.

Be Flexible

As discussed, the nature of all things is to change. This includes our selves, our Persons and even our nature because all phenomena are impermanent. We spend our lives trying to interfere with this natural process to protect our Persons' needs. Often, we have rigidly held beliefs about the way things should be that are at odds with the changing nature of reality. This rigidity leaves us vulnerable to becoming maladaptive to our environment and events that unfold in our lives. Things that are rigid tend to be brittle and susceptible to breaking when under stress. From an evolutionary perspective, species that are not flexible are at risk of extinction. Life on Earth has evolved to be flexible and this flexibility is present in our nature. In self-obsession, we become unadaptable and this makes us vulnerable to change. By cultivating a more flexible mindset, we can better adapt to the inevitable changes in our lives and maintain a state of harmony with the Tao. Embracing flexibility helps us reduce resistance to life's uncertainties and teaches us to flow with change rather than fight against it.

"*Yield and remain whole. Bend and remain straight.*" Laozi

Practising Flexibility

1. Change one routine habit each week. For example, take a different route to work or try a new food or recipe.

2. Whenever you make plans, have a Plan B to switch to if things don't go as expected.
3. Make plans that are vague! Perhaps it's a spontaneous trip or day out. Adapt to the situation as it unfolds and observe your creativity and ability to problem solve.
4. Reflect on the impact that being flexible has on your ability to navigate change. What other areas of your life can you approach more flexibly?

Balance Action With Non-Action

Self-obsession can make us feel like we constantly need to take action. Often, this involves taking steps to resist or protect ourselves from change or actively striving for things that we believe will improve our selves and how we see our Persons. Doing nothing can feel like we're not being proactive or productive, that we're letting life pass us by. Being passive can make us feel anxious as we believe it increases the risk of events unfolding in undesirable ways. We do not trust life to work out but see our lives as a series of obstacles we must carefully navigate to reach our preferred destination. Our lives become a constant struggle requiring continuous vigilance to avoid negative outcomes and become the Person we *should* be.

This endless need to be doing is a symptom of self-obsession and causes us a great deal of unnecessary stress and exhaustion. Living in accordance with our nature is referred to in Taoism as "Wu Wei", which translates to "effortless action" or "doing without doing". This means that actions are performed without strain or excessive effort, aligning seamlessly with the natural flow of life. In Wu Wei, we engage in our day-to-day tasks in a way that feels natural and unforced. We learn to act when it is necessary and rest when it is appropriate, trusting life will unfold as it should.

Rather than trying to direct every aspect of our lives, we allow ourselves to become receptive to the rhythms and patterns of nature, moving with them in a harmonious and balanced way. This allows us to accept our present reality as it is and let go of any rigid ideas about how things should be.

"*Rushing into action leads to failure, grasping leads to loss and forcing something to completion will ruin it.*" Laozi

Practising Non-Action

1. List areas in your life where you experience frequent stress. Identify the specific self-element and note how and why it feels like such a struggle.
2. Alongside each self-element, make a note of your underlying motivations that are driving you to engage in these behaviours. Why is it so important to you? What need are you looking to fulfil?
3. For each struggle, reflect on whether your actions are fulfilling the needs you've identified or if they are contributing to further stress.
4. Choose one self-element where you feel action may not be the best approach. Consciously decide not to engage in your usual behaviour and observe what happens. Notice any change in your stress levels and whether the situation resolves itself.
5. After practising non-action, reflect on how it felt to step back rather than intervene. Did the issue work itself out? Were there any unexpected benefits gained by not interfering?

Closing Thoughts

As we have discussed, when we let go of the self and our Person we let go of something artificial that has been obscuring who we really are. Most of us spend our lives striving to be the Person we think we *need* to be, that society says we *should* be. Unfortunately, this serves to take us further from our true nature. We become actors in roles that don't suit us and then spend our lives trying to learn someone else's script. Self-obsession is a conditioned state of constant struggle that is unnecessary and painful. The path to freedom is a simple one. Be what comes naturally, do what feels right. Free yourself from ambition, let go of attachment to material things. Strive only to be who you are and treat others as extensions of your being. This is the great effortless, aimless and compassionate path that will take you beyond self-obsession.

REFLECTION

What are you able to give up?
What are you willing to unlearn?
If the answer is everything, the whole world is yours.
Start with something.
Surround yourself with those who see it.
In this moment, what is truly lacking?

"Happiness is the absence of striving for happiness."

Zhuangzi

FINAL THOUGHTS

I used to think I was a nobody and was desperate to be somebody. Then I believed I was somebody and was terrified of being a nobody. When I became a nobody, I grieved the somebody I used to be. Both the nobody and the somebody were called Tom. Identifying as somebody, I felt anxious. Identifying as a nobody, I felt depressed. But when I identify as neither, I feel free. To overcome self-obsession is to escape the false dichotomy that exists between who we are and who we think we should be. Beyond this dualistic misconception is who we have always been.

Self-obsession is an obsession with an idea. It is a rigid belief that our identity is as real as the ground beneath our feet. This belief has been reinforced our entire lives because it's a belief shared by the rest of humanity and is deeply engrained within the societies in which we live. Each of us believes in the metaphysical narrative of our Person because we think it's the only thing we have. Few of us dare to consider that this Person and the self it attaches to are nothing more than fantasies. Of course, not all fantasies are unhelpful. One only has to look to literature and art to see the value of fantasy. However, if a fantasy fills our lives with pain, would this fantasy not be better described as a nightmare?

Self-obsession is the nightmare responsible for the psychological distress we experience. The problem is that most of us don't know we are dreaming. We wake up each morning believing that we have opened our eyes to reality when we have merely changed from one dream state to another. The cruel irony is that when we are asleep, we are free from the self-obsessed nature of our waking life but are blissfully unaware of this freedom. Conversely, when we wake up, we're immediately trapped within the confines of self-obsession, helplessly unaware that we're trapped. As I write this I'm reminded of a period of my life when my anxiety was at its worst. Each night, I would lie in bed for hours, tormented by worry. Eventually, exhausted, I would begin to fall asleep. However, as I started to drift off, I'd suddenly find myself wide awake again, heart racing and gasping for air. It was a horrible experience that would happen many times each night before I finally fell asleep. I'd lie there helplessly, wondering why my brain tormented me – inviting me to the cusp of the deep sleep that I desperately craved, only to rip it away in such a terrifying manner. Was the constant stress I experienced during the day not enough? Did my brain need to torture me through the night, too?

I read various plausible explanations for what was causing this problem. The most convincing was the theory that high levels of anxiety meant my sympathetic nervous system responsible for fight and flight was overactive at night and struggled to surrender to its parasympathetic cousin that's more active during rest. The physiological changes associated with falling asleep were interpreted by my anxious brain as potential threats, triggering the sudden panic that kept me trapped in my wakened state. This is a compelling neurological explanation but I now wonder how much of this problem was caused by self-obsession. Could it have been that I was so desperately clinging to the Person I was trying to be that my mind refused to let him go, even at night? Was my attachment such that sleep represented a loss of control that the observing "I" of conscious awareness was unwilling to accept?

The more I understand self-obsession, the more I can see the effects it's had on my life. I spent so many years pointing the finger of blame elsewhere that I failed to see *the* problem beneath the other problems I was frantically trying to solve. Self-obsession commits the perfect crime because it masquerades as so many other things and hides itself behind the greatest deception in the history of mankind – the Person. We live our lives pursuing the ideals that self-obsession promises, only to realize that they're empty promises. The more we chase happiness, the less happy we feel. The more we chase success, the more elusive it becomes. Self-obsession convinces us to follow The Road of Great Purpose but it's a road that leads us further away from who we really are.

When I began walking along The Road of Emptiness, it was not by choice or from a spiritual awakening or moment of enlightenment. I started this path kicking and screaming, unable to let go of the life I desperately wanted. It felt like everyone else was on the right path and I was going in the opposite direction. However, the depression I was experiencing was not caused by The Road of Emptiness. It was caused by my attachment to The Road of Great Purpose. Hope and hopelessness, success and failure, meaning and apathy are all found on The Road of Great Purpose. On The Road of Emptiness, there are none of these things. There is no fixed destination, no opportunities to take a wrong turn and nothing that needs to be achieved. The Road of Emptiness promises nothing and provides everything. It's the only way to be free, no matter how much our self-obsessed minds tell us otherwise.

I am still self-obsessed. A part of me still clings to the life I used to have. There are moments when I am working as a therapist when I wish I was still a practising doctor. The loss of my medical career hit me hard and I'm still processing the grief. But I now know the problem. I know I over-identified with my career as a means of fulfilling a deep psychological need within me. It was a need to belong, a need to be recognized as good enough. Now I know who this need belongs to I have the power to choose how I respond to it.

172

I can either be true to myself or a slave to my Person. I have been a slave long enough and I deserve to be free. Every day, The Road of Emptiness feels more familiar. Every day, I become less self-obsessed. Every day, I get closer to myself.

You deserve to be happy,
You deserve to be free.
Find where the finite meets the infinite,
And where the two become one.
I'll meet you there.
On The Road of Great Emptiness,
We can share the journey home.

ENDNOTES

1 These categories, often called the "Big 5", were refined and popularized by key contributors such as Gordon Allport, who laid the groundwork for trait theory, and Paul Costa and Robert McCrae, who developed the NEO Personality Inventory, a widely used assessment tool based on these traits.

2 Srivastava, S., John, O.P., Gosling, S.D. and Potter, J., "Development of personality in early and middle adulthood: Set like plaster or persistent change?", *Journal of Personality and Social Psychology*, 84 (13), 2003, pp.1041-1053

3 National Institute for Clinical Excellence (NICE) 2019, *Eating disorders: Prevalence*, NICE Clinical Knowledge Summaries. 'Should we be surprised that about eight per cent of the global population will experience an eating disorder in their lifetimes? Author unknown, "Eating disorders: How common is it?", *National Institute for Health and Care Excellence*, 2024, https://cks.nice.org.uk/topics/eating-disorders/background-information/prevalence/

4   Anderson, F.B., Djugum, M.E.T., Sjastad, V.S., Pallesen, S., "The prevalence of workaholism: a systematic review and meta-analysis", *Frontiers in Psychology*, 2023, www.frontiersin.org/journals/psychology/articles/ 10.3389/fpsyg.2023.1252373/full

5   The CBT theory and techniques detailed in this chapter and subsequent chapters are based on the foundational work of Aaron Beck, *Cognitive Therapy of Depression* (1979) and the work of his daughter, Judith Beck, *Cognitive Behavioural Therapy: Basics and Beyond* (2021).

6   Norcross, J.C. and Lambert, M.J. 2018 *Psychotherapy Relationships That Work: Volume 3. Oxford University Press,* Oxford, 2018.

7   The specific English translation of the Tao Te Ching used for reference in this chapter was masterfully written by Stephen Mitchell. This includes the translated quotes attributed to Laozi. *Tao Te Ching: An Illustrated Journey* Frances Lincoln; UK ed. edition, 1999.

ACKNOWLEDGEMENTS

To my agent, Hattie, thank you for taking a chance on me and for believing in the importance of the themes explored in this book.

To my editor, Ella at Watkins, thank you for giving me the freedom to write this book my way while ensuring it stayed true to its purpose and connected with readers.

To my patients, whose experiences continue to inspire and deepen my understanding of the human condition—this book would not exist without you.

And finally, to the wider teams at The Blair Partnership and Watkins, thank you for your invaluable support behind the scenes.

ABOUT THE AUTHOR

Dr Tom Davies studied Biology at Warwick University before training as a doctor at King's College London. He has worked in primary and secondary care, including General Practice and Psychiatry, and is currently practising as a therapist.

Drawing on his own psychological challenges, Tom brings a personal and compassionate perspective to his work, often helping patients navigate struggles he has faced himself.

For over a decade, Tom has explored psychology and philosophy, focusing on the Eastern spiritual traditions of Buddhism, Taoism and Hinduism. His insights are shaped by this exploration, as well as his experiences working with mental health patients, his own spiritual practice and many long-distance hiking adventures across Europe.

0| 14
√